Study Skills
Green

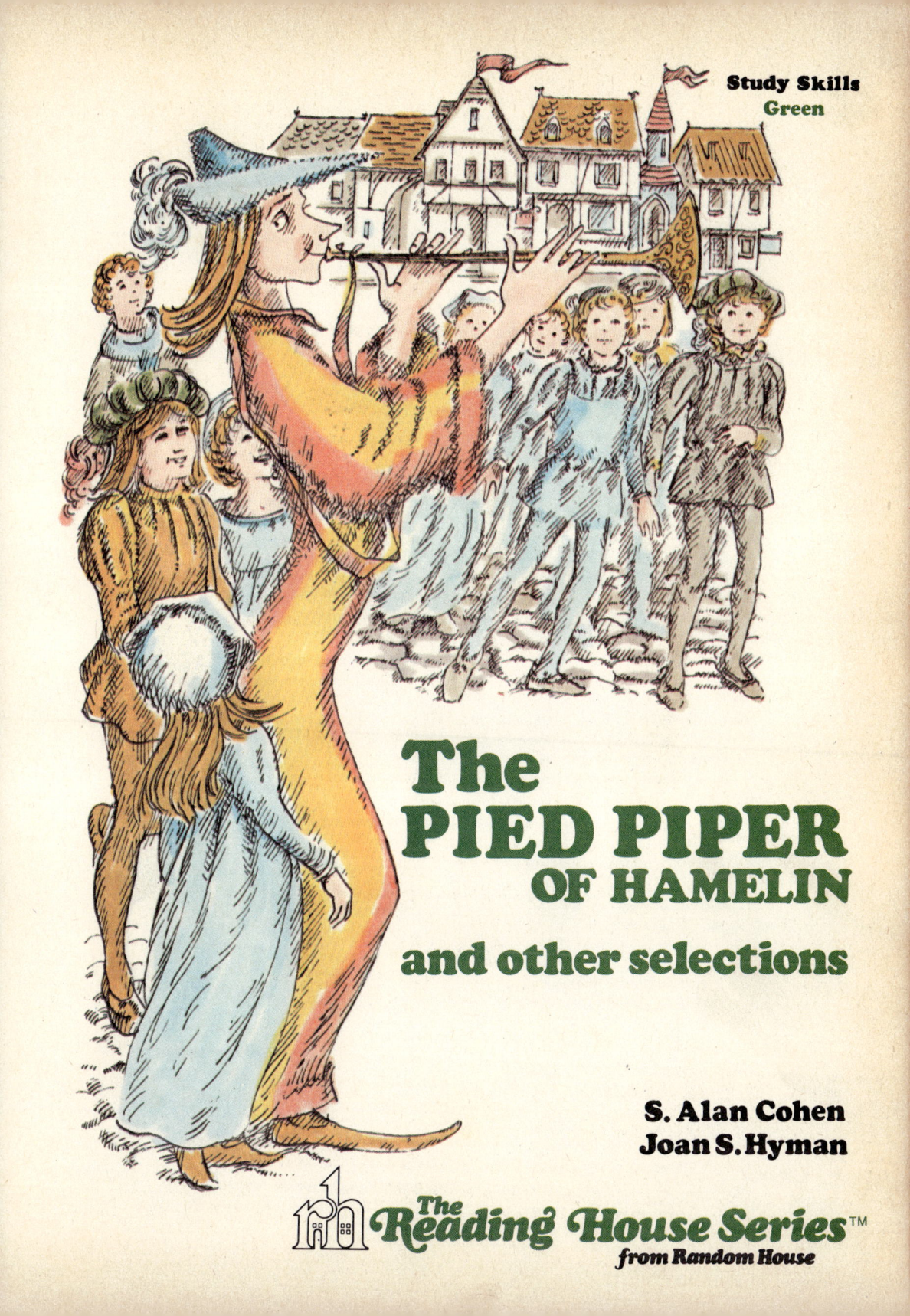

The PIED PIPER OF HAMELIN
and other selections

S. Alan Cohen
Joan S. Hyman

The Reading House Series
from Random House

ACKNOWLEDGMENTS

Grateful acknowledgment is made to the authors, publishers, agents, and individuals for their permission to use the following materials:

Selection on page 21, "Emergency!" by Nick Pease. Used by permission.

Selection on page 83, "Uptown Hero" by Nick Pease. Used by permission.

Selection on page 88, "Doctor of the Mind" by Nick Pease. Used by permission.

"The Pied Piper of Hamelin" on page 2 from THE SELECTED POETRY OF ROBERT BROWNING, edited by Kenneth L. Knickerbocker. Copyright 1951 by Random House, Inc. Reprinted by permission of Random House, Inc.

Selection on page 14 from DANDELIONS DON'T BITE, by Leone Adelson. Copyright © 1972 by Leone Adelson. Reprinted by permission of Pantheon Books, a division of Random House, Inc.

Selection on page 19 from THE KAHLIL GIBRAN DIARY FOR 1976, by Kahlil Gibran. Copyright © 1972 by Alfred A. Knopf, Inc. Reprinted by permission of the publisher.

Selection on page 28 from BATS: WINGS IN THE NIGHT, by Patricia Lauber. Copyright © 1968 by Patricia Lauber. Reprinted by permission of Random House, Inc.

Selection on page 31 from PANTHER'S MOON, by Ruskin Bond. Copyright © 1969 by Ruskin Bond. Reprinted by permission of Random House, Inc.

"Dear March, Come In" on page 39 from THE COMPLETE POEMS OF EMILY DICKINSON, edited by Thomas H. Johnson. Reprinted by permission of Little, Brown and Company, The Belknap Press of Harvard University Press and the Trustees of Amherst College. Copyright © 1951, 1955 by the President and Fellows of Harvard College.

Selection on page 41 from BURNISH ME BRIGHT, by Julia Cunningham. Copyright © 1970 by Julia Cunningham. Reprinted by permission of Pantheon Books, a division of Random House, Inc. and of William Heinemann Ltd.

Selections on page 47 from COLLECTED SHORTER POEMS 1927-1957, by W.H. Auden. Copyright © 1966 by W.H. Auden. Reprinted by permission of Random House, Inc.

Excerpt of "Shorts" on page 47 from THANK YOU, FOG: LAST POEMS BY W.H. AUDEN. Copyright © 1972, 1973 by W.H. Auden. Copyright © 1973, 1974 by the Estate of W.H. Auden. Reprinted by permission of Random House, Inc.

Selections on pages 49-52 from THE WISDOM OF CHINA AND INDIA, edited by Lin Yutang. Copyright 1942 by Random House, Inc. Reprinted by permission of Random House, Inc. and of Michael Joseph Limited.

"An Introduction to Dogs" on page 54 from I'M A STRANGER HERE MYSELF, by Ogden Nash. Copyright 1938 by Ogden Nash. Reprinted by permission of Little, Brown and Company and of J.M. Dent and Sons.

"The Rhinoceros" on page 55 from VERSES FROM 1929 ON, by Ogden Nash. Copyright 1933 by Ogden Nash. Originally appeared in the *New Yorker*. Reprinted by permission of Little, Brown and Company and of J.M. Dent and Sons.

Acknowledgments continued on page 92

Library of Congress Cataloging in Publication Data

```
Cohen, S. Alan
    The Pied Piper of Hamelin, and other selections.

  (The Reading house series from Random House : Study skills (green))
    SUMMARY: Eighteen reading selections which develop various basic reading skills. Includes follow-
up activities.
    1. Readers—1950-     [1. Readers]
I. Hyman, Joan S., joint author.    II. Title.
PE1121.C545      428'.6      76-48059
ISBN 0-394-04434-7
```

Copyright © 1977 by Random House, Inc.

All rights reserved under International and Pan-American Copyright Conventions. Published in the United States by Random House, Inc., New York, and simultaneously in Canada by Random House of Canada Limited, Toronto.

Manufactured in the United States of America
ISBN 0-394-04434-7

CONTENTS

73 page **2**

The Pied Piper of Hamelin

74 page **14**

Dandelions Don't Bite

75 page **19**

Aphorisms

76 page **21**

Emergency!

77 page **28**

Vampire Bats

78 page **31**

Wondering Why

For each Instructional Objective (I-O) the student masters in Tests and Tasks for Study Skills (Green), there is an appropriate selection in this RH Reader. The I-O numeral listed in the Contents directs the student to the particular reading selection and its follow-up activities.

79 page **36**

To Every Thing There Is a Season

80 page **39**

Dear March, Come In!

81 page **41**

Auguste, the Mime

82 page **47**

Faces

83 page **49**

Chinese Parables

84 page **54**

Animal Crackers

| 85 | page 57 |

Obsession

| 86 | page 63 |

Trillions

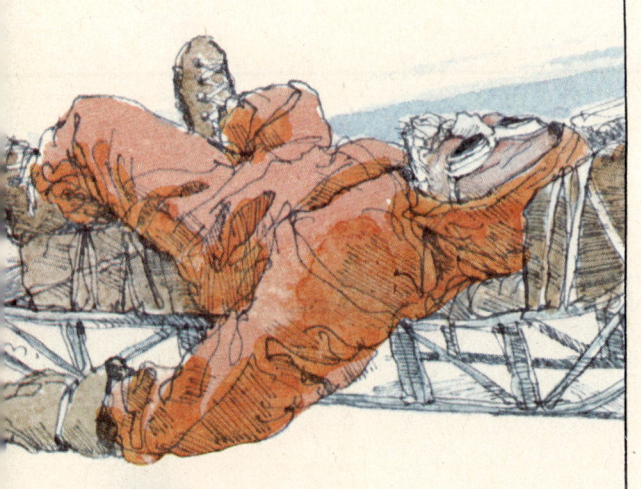

| 87 | page 76 |

Shadow of Death

| 88 | page 80 |

Mind Your Manners

| 89 | page 83 |

Uptown Hero

| 90 | page 88 |

Doctor of the Mind

THE PIED PIPER OF HAMELIN

by Robert Browning

Rats! Rats! Millions of rats! That was the problem in Hamelin, a German town, several hundred years ago. (Robert Browning wrote this story in verse about one hundred years ago.) According to legend, the Pied Piper had a unique way of solving the rat problem. But can you imagine what happened when the greedy town officials did not keep their promise to pay the Piper?

I

HAMELIN TOWN's in Brunswick,
By famous Hanover city;
The river Weser, deep and wide,
Washes its wall on the southern side;
A pleasanter spot you never spied;
But, when begins my ditty,
Almost five hundred years ago,
To see the townsfolk suffer so
From vermin, was a pity.

II

Rats!
They fought the dogs and killed the cats,
And bit the babies in the cradles,
And ate the cheeses out of the vats,
And licked the soup from the cooks' own ladles,
Split open the kegs of salted sprats,
Made nests inside men's Sunday hats,
And even spoiled the women's chats
By drowning their speaking
With shrieking and squeaking
In fifty different sharps and flats.

III

At last the people in a body
To the Town Hall came flocking:
"'Tis clear," cried they, "our Mayor's a noddy;
And as for our Corporation—shocking
To think we buy gowns lined with ermine
For dolts that can't or won't determine
What's best to rid us of our vermin!
You hope, because you're old and obese,
To find in the furry civic robe ease?
Rouse up, sirs! Give your brains a racking
To find the remedy we're lacking,
Or, sure as fate, we'll send you packing!"
At this the Mayor and Corporation
Quaked with a mighty consternation.

IV

An hour they sat in council,
At length the Mayor broke silence:
"For a guilder I'd my ermine gown sell,
I wish I were a mile hence!
It's easy to bid one rack one's brain—
I'm sure my poor head aches again,
I've scratched it so, and all in vain.
Oh for a trap, a trap, a trap!"
Just as he said this, what should hap
At the chamber door a gentle tap?
"Bless us," cried the Mayor, "what's that?"
(With the Corporation as he sat,
Looking little though wondrous fat;
Nor blighter was his eye, nor moister
Than a too-long opened oyster,
Save when at noon his paunch grew mutinous
For a plate of turtle green and glutinous)
"Only a scraping of shoes on the mat?
Anything like the sound of a rat
Makes my heart go pit-a-pat!"

V

"Come in!"—the Mayor cried, looking bigger:
And in did come the strangest figure!
His queer long coat from heel to head
Was half of yellow and half of red.
And he himself was tall and thin,
With sharp blue eyes, each like a pin,
And light loose hair, yet swarthy skin,
No tuft on cheek nor beard on chin,
But lips where smiles went out and in;
There was no guessing his kith and kin:
And nobody could enough admire
The tall man and his quaint attire.
Quoth one: "It's as my great-grandsire,
Starting up at the Trump of Doom's tone,
Had walked his way from his painted tombstone!"

VI

He advanced to the council-table:
And, "Please your honors," said he, "I'm able,
By means of a secret charm, to draw
All creatures living beneath the sun,
That creep or swim or fly or run,
After me so as you never saw!
And I chiefly use my charm
On creatures that do people harm,
The mole and toad and newt and viper;
And people call me the Pied Piper."

(And here they noticed round his neck
A scarf of red and yellow stripe,
To match with his coat of the self-same cheque;
And at the scarf's end hung a pipe;
And his fingers, they noticed, were ever straying
As if impatient to be playing
Upon this pipe, as low it dangled
Over his vesture so old-fangled.)
"Yet," said he, "poor piper I am,
In Tartary I freed the Cham,
Last June, from his huge swarms of gnats;
I eased in Asia the Nizam
Of a monstrous brood of vampyre-bats:
And as for what your brain bewilders,
If I can rid your town of rats
Will you give me a thousand guilders?"
"One? fifty thousand!"—was the exclamation
Of the astonished Mayor and Corporation.

VII

Into the street the Piper stept,
Smiling first a little smile,
As if he knew what magic slept
In his quiet pipe the while;
Then, like a musical adept,
To blow the pipe his lips he wrinkled,
And green and blue his sharp eyes twinkled,
Like a candle-flame where salt is sprinkled;
And ere three shrill notes the pipe uttered,
You heard as if an army muttered;
And the muttering grew to a grumbling;
And the grumbling grew to a mighty rumbling;
And out of the houses the rats came tumbling.
Great rats, small rats, lean rats, brawny rats,
Brown rats, black rats, gray rats, tawny rats,
Grave old plodders, gay young friskers,

Fathers, mothers, uncles, cousins,
Cocking tails and pricking whiskers,
Families by tens and dozens,
Brothers, sisters, husbands, wives—
Followed the Piper for their lives.
From street to street he piped advancing,
And step for step they followed dancing,
Until they came to the river Weser,
Wherein all plunged and perished!
—Save one who, stout as Julius Caesar,
Swam across and lived to carry
(As he, the manuscript he cherished)
To Rat-land home his commentary:
Which was, "At the first shrill notes of the pipe,
I heard a sound as of scraping tripe,
And putting apples, wondrous ripe,
Into a cider-press's gripe:

And a moving away of pickle-tub-boards,
And a leaving ajar of conserve-cupboards,
And a drawing the corks of train-oil-flasks,
And a breaking the hoops of butter-casks:
And it seemed as if a voice
(Sweeter far than by harp or by psaltery
Is breathed) called out, 'Oh rats, rejoice!
The world is grown to one vast drysaltery!
So munch on, crunch on, take your nuncheon,
Breakfast, supper, dinner, luncheon!'
And just as a bulky sugar-puncheon,
All ready staved, like a great sun shone
Glorious scarce an inch before me,
Just as methought it said, 'Come, bore me!'
—I found the Weser rolling o'er me."

VIII

You should have heard the Hamelin people
Ringing the bells till they rocked the steeple.
"Go," cried the Mayor, "and get long poles,
Poke out the nests and block up the holes!
Consult with carpenters and builders,
And leave in our town not even a trace
Of the rats!"—when suddenly, up the face
Of the Piper perked in the market-place,
With a, "First, if you please, my thousand guilders!"

IX

A thousand guilders! The Mayor looked blue;
So did the Corporation too.
For council dinners made rare havoc
With Claret, Moselle, Vin-de-Grave, Hock;
And half the money would replenish
Their cellar's biggest butt with Rhenish.
To pay this sum to a wandering fellow
With a gipsy coat of red and yellow!
"Beside," quoth the Mayor with a knowing wink,
"Our business was done at the river's brink;
We saw with our eyes the vermin sink,
And what's dead can't come to life, I think.
So, friend, we're not the folks to shrink
From the duty of giving you something to drink,
And a matter of money to put in your poke;
But as for the guilders, what we spoke
Of them, as you very well know, was in joke.
Beside, our losses have made us thrifty.
A thousand guilders! Come, take fifty!"

X

The Piper's face fell, and he cried
"No trifling! I can't wait, beside!
I've promised to visit by dinnertime
Bagdat, and accept the prime
Of the Head-Cook's pottage, all he's rich in,
For having left, in the Caliph's kitchen,
Of a nest of scorpions no survivor:
With him I proved no bargain-driver,
With you, don't think I'll bate a stiver!
And folks who put me in a passion
May find me pipe after another fashion."

XI

"How?" cried the Mayor, "d'ye think I brook
Being worse treated than a Cook?

Insulted by a lazy ribald
With idle pipe and vesture piebald?
You threaten us, fellow? Do your worst,
Blow your pipe there till you burst!"

XII

Once more he stept into the street
And to his lips again
Laid his long pipe of smooth straight cane;
And ere he blew three notes (such sweet
Soft notes as yet musician's cunning
Never gave the enraptured air)
There was a rustling that seemed like a bustling
Of merry crowds justling at pitching and hustling,
Small feet were pattering, wooden shoes clattering,
Little hands clapping and little tongues chattering,
And, like fowls in a farm-yard when barley is scattering,
Out came the children running.
All the little boys and girls,
With rosy cheeks and flaxen curls,
And sparkling eyes and teeth like pearls,
Tripping and skipping, ran merrily after
The wonderful music with shouting and laughter.

XIII

The Mayor was dumb, and the Council stood
As if they were changed into blocks of wood,
Unable to move a step, or cry
To the children merrily skipping by,
—Could only follow with the eye
That joyous crowd at the Piper's back.
But how the Mayor was on the rack,
And the wretched Council's bosoms beat,
As the Piper turned from the High Street
To where the Weser rolled its waters
Right in the way of their sons and daughters!
However he turned from South to West,

And to Koppelberg Hill his steps addressed,
And after him the children pressed;
Great was the joy in every breast.
"He never can cross that mighty top!
He's forced to let the piping drop,
And we shall see our children stop!"
When, lo, as they reached the mountain-side,
A wondrous portal opened wide,
As if a cavern was suddenly hollowed;
And the Piper advanced and the children followed,
And when all were in to the very last,
The door in the mountain-side shut fast.
Did I say, all? No! One was lame,
And could not dance the whole of the way;
And in after years, if you would blame
His sadness, he was used to say,—

"It's dull in our town since my playmates left!
I can't forget that I'm bereft
Of all the pleasant sights they see,
Which the Piper also promised me.
For he led us, he said, to a joyous land,
Joining the town and just at hand,
Where waters gushed and fruit-trees grew
And flowers put forth a fairer hue,
And everything was strange and new;
The sparrows were brighter than peacocks here,
And their dogs outran our fallow deer,
And honey-bees had lost their stings,
And horses were born with eagles' wings:
And just as I became assured
My lame foot would be speedily cured,
The music stopped and I stood still,
And found myself outside the hill,
Left alone against my will,
To go now limping as before,
And never hear of that country more!"

XIV

Alas, alas for Hamelin!
There came into many a burgher's pate
A text which says that heaven's gate
Opes to the rich at as easy rate
As the needle's eye takes a camel in!
The Mayor sent East, West, North and South,
To offer the Piper, by word of mouth,
Wherever it was men's lot to find him,
Silver and gold to his heart's content,
If he'd only return the way he went,
And bring the children behind him.
But when they saw 'twas a lost endeavor,
And Piper and dancers were gone forever,
They made a decree that lawyers never

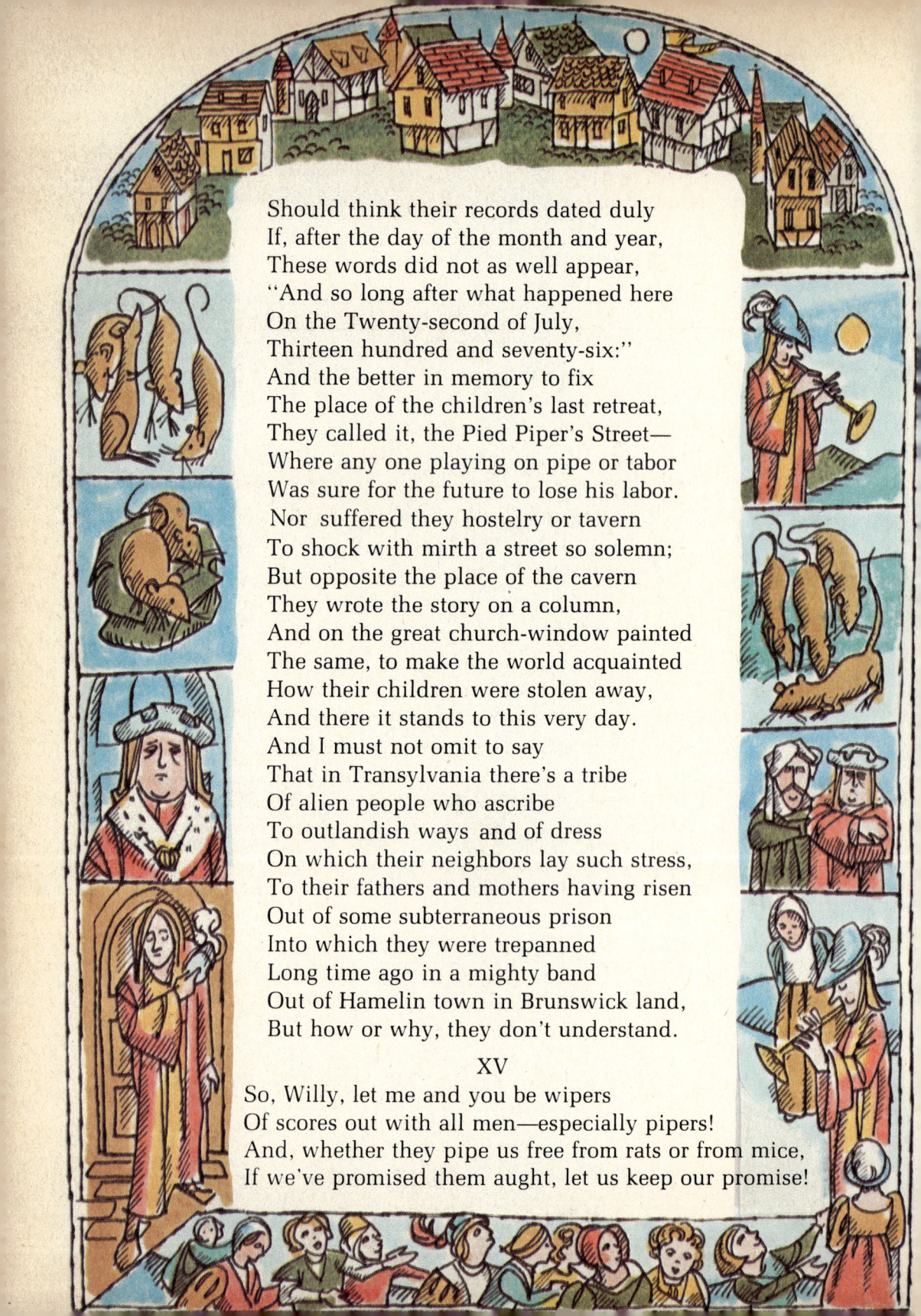

Should think their records dated duly
If, after the day of the month and year,
These words did not as well appear,
"And so long after what happened here
On the Twenty-second of July,
Thirteen hundred and seventy-six:"
And the better in memory to fix
The place of the children's last retreat,
They called it, the Pied Piper's Street—
Where any one playing on pipe or tabor
Was sure for the future to lose his labor.
Nor suffered they hostelry or tavern
To shock with mirth a street so solemn;
But opposite the place of the cavern
They wrote the story on a column,
And on the great church-window painted
The same, to make the world acquainted
How their children were stolen away,
And there it stands to this very day.
And I must not omit to say
That in Transylvania there's a tribe
Of alien people who ascribe
To outlandish ways and of dress
On which their neighbors lay such stress,
To their fathers and mothers having risen
Out of some subterraneous prison
Into which they were trepanned
Long time ago in a mighty band
Out of Hamelin town in Brunswick land,
But how or why, they don't understand.

XV

So, Willy, let me and you be wipers
Of scores out with all men—especially pipers!
And, whether they pipe us free from rats or from mice,
If we've promised them aught, let us keep our promise!

THE PIED PIPER OF HAMELIN

(pages 2-12)

1. What is the moral of this tale?

2. In a drysaltery, meat is dried and salted to preserve it. What did the Piper's tune tell the rats with these words:
   The world is grown to one vast drysaltery!
   So munch on, crunch on, take your nuncheon,
   Breakfast, supper, dinner, luncheon!

3. Choose the best definition of *Mayor* in this quote:
   An hour they sat in council,
   At length the Mayor broke silence

   A. elder B. treasurer

   may·or (mā′ər), *n.* the chief official of a city or town. [from the Latin word *major* "greater, elder"]

4. Choose the best definition of *poke* for this quote:
   And a matter of money to put in your poke

   poke¹ (pōk), *v.*, **poked, pok·ing.** 1. to prod or push with something pointed, such as a finger, elbow, or stick: *to poke someone in the ribs.*
   poke² (pōk), *n.* a bag or sack: a word used esp. in the South and Midwest. [from a Middle English word, which comes from Old French *poque* "bag"]
   poke³ (pōk), *n.* a bonnet with a projecting brim at the front, framing the face. [special use of *poke¹*]

ANSWERS

1. Pay what you owe and keep your promises.
2. The tune promised the rats all the food they could eat.
3. A
4. a bag or sack

DANDELIONS DON'T BITE

The Story of Words

from the book by Leone Adelson

Who said the first word? What was it? How did it sound? *Nobody knows.*

There are no old phonograph records or sound films or videotapes to tell us. The beginnings of the spoken word are a mystery.

Language detectives, or linguists, have been hunting for clues to this mystery for hundreds of years. They have listened to the talk of people living in lonely places from the North Pole to the South Pole. They have even studied the first sounds made by tiny babies. So far, there are no sure answers. But there are many good guesses.

Whenever a great number of people decide that certain sounds would make a good, useful word, then those sounds become a new word.

Suppose all the people in your neighborhood decide to say, "Orningmoo Oodgoo" instead of "Good Morning." Then suppose other neighborhoods decide that they like the new greeting too, and soon thousands of people in the city and across the country are saying it.

"Orningmoo Oodgoo, Mrs. Jones."

"Orningmoo Oodgoo, Mrs. Smith."

Soon "Orningmoo Oodgoo" finds its way into newspapers, books, television, and radio. You may be sure that it will soon be found in the dictionaries too. A new expression has been adopted by the people.

Tracing words back to their beginnings is a little like following a maze. Sometimes you think you're on the right track only to find that it's going in the wrong direction. Back you go to make a new start, with another dictionary or word book to help you.

Take the words *pupil, puppy,* and *puppet,* for instance. They have the same Latin ancestor, *pupilla,* a little doll or small person. A class of *pupils* are not just little dolls. But pupil has another meaning too, of course

—the center of your eye. To find out what a little doll has to do with the pupil of your eye you must get someone to stand in front of you in a good light. Look deep into his or her eyes and what do you see? Yourself, of course! But how small you look! Like a little doll. Now that you know *pupilla,* it should not be hard for you to find out how *puppy* and *puppet* came to be related.

Here are some more word cousins and their stories: *clock, cloak.* You must go way back to ancient France to trace these two English words. At that time, every village had a bell which could be heard everywhere. It rang every hour to give the time. The French word for bell is *cloche.* When timepieces at last began to find their way into village homes, people still called them *cloches.* When the word came into English, *cloche* became *clock.* What could all this have to do with *cloak,* clock's cousin? It's easy to see now that people wrapped in long, warm capes looked like bells. But this time when *cloche* came into English, it made a slight change and became *cloak,* a bell-shaped cape.

Other words have to be coaxed to tell us about themselves and where they come from. *Dandelion:* The name of this little yellow, shaggy flower that grows like a weed, did not settle down to its present spelling until it had been back and forth between France and England several times, centuries ago. From the sharp, jagged edges of its leaves it got the name "Lion's tooth." When the French invaded England, many English words took on French accents. The little lion's tooth plant became the *dent-de-lion* (tooth-of-the-lion). Then it took on an English accent and became *dandelion.* As you can see, *dent* means tooth. Does that give you a clue to some other words, having to do with teeth, that have *dent* in them?

If anyone asks you if you speak any other languages beside English, you may honestly say "Yes, many!" All these words, used all the time, are foreign ones, with some slight changes in spelling: *Kimono*—a Japanese housecoat. *Algebra*—a form of arithmetic first used in Arabia. *Bamboo* and *ketchup*—a plant and a sauce from the Indonesian islands. *So long*—in Malay this form of good-by is *salang*. *Chimpanzee*—a word from the Congo in Africa.

Who does not like to eat! Everyone does. That is why so many of the foreign words in the English language seem to be for good things to eat. Many of the wonderful mouth-watering foods from Italy alone can make a delicious dinner. (If you're hungry you had better skip this part.)

First, the *antipasto*—what you eat before (*anti-*) the main meal (*pasto*) to give you a good appetite—*pizza*, and spicy sausages like *salami, bologna,* and *pepperoni*. Now the soup—*minestrone*, "the big soup," thick with beans and vegetables. Next comes the *pasta*. Pasta is nothing but a paste made of flour, eggs and water, but to the Italians and now to us it is our *spaghetti, macaroni,* and *ravioli*. If you have room for dessert, have some Italian ice cream—*spumoni* or *tortoni*.

French cooking is known the world over, and many French dishes are now part of American cooking: *soupe*, which we spell without the e, *mayonnaise, omelette, fricassee, tartes* (tarts), *toste* (toast), *bonbons*. The French cook who makes all these good things is the *chef*, the chief or head cook in the kitchen.

The Germans and the Dutch gave us *hamburgers* and *frankfurters*, from the German cities of Hamburg and Frankfurt.

Our close neighbors, the Spanish-speaking people of Mexico, have given us hot *tamales, chile con carne, tapioca, vanilla, bananas,* the *barbecue* way of cooking, and the *cafeteria*.

The English language is beginning to pay back for some of the words we have borrowed. The word-traffic across the oceans is now becoming a two-way street instead of a one-way street. That is because foreign countries are using some of our words, as we

Russians pay for avtomobils by chek.

have used theirs. They may not spell them quite the same way, or even say them as we do, but it's easy to recognize them just the same.

Can you recognize *futbol* and *beisbol?* The whole world plays them! Many Japanese use *hankechis* to wipe their noses, *pen* and *inki* to write letters, and a *naifu* and *foku* to cut their food and eat their dinners.

The Russians take *fotografs*, drive *avtomobils*, pay their bills by *chek*, and go to the *gospital* when they are sick.

If you like to sleep outdoors you can find *campings* signs all over Europe. If you like hot dogs, that's what they're called in Europe too! So are sandwiches.

So if you travel abroad and if you speak only English, don't be afraid—you will not be as much of a stranger as you might think!

For century after century after century a great treasure of words has been building up. Most treasures are locked up and put away for safekeeping. But not language! The more that treasure is used the longer it lasts. Whenever you use a word, you help to keep it alive. Words that are not used disappear from our language, and new ones come along to take their places.

A poet has said, "Language is made by the people." And it's what people say that counts!

DANDELIONS DON'T BITE
The Story of Words

(pages 14-17)

1. What is a *linguist*?

2. When does a new expression that someone invents become a new word?

3. From which countries do these words come?
    A. mayonnaise, omelette
    B. vanilla, banana

4. Why must we often refer to other languages when we trace the meanings of English words?

5. What words can you find in the dictionary that begin with *dent* and have something to do with teeth?

6. Name the base word for each of the following:
     invaded   meaning   detectives

ANSWERS

1. A linguist studies the origins of the sounds and words of a language.
2. after many other people have used it
3. A. France   B. Mexico
4. Many English words have come from other languages.
5. Dental, dentifrice, dentist, dentistry, denture are some of the words that begin with *dent* and have something to do with teeth.
6. invade, mean, detect

18

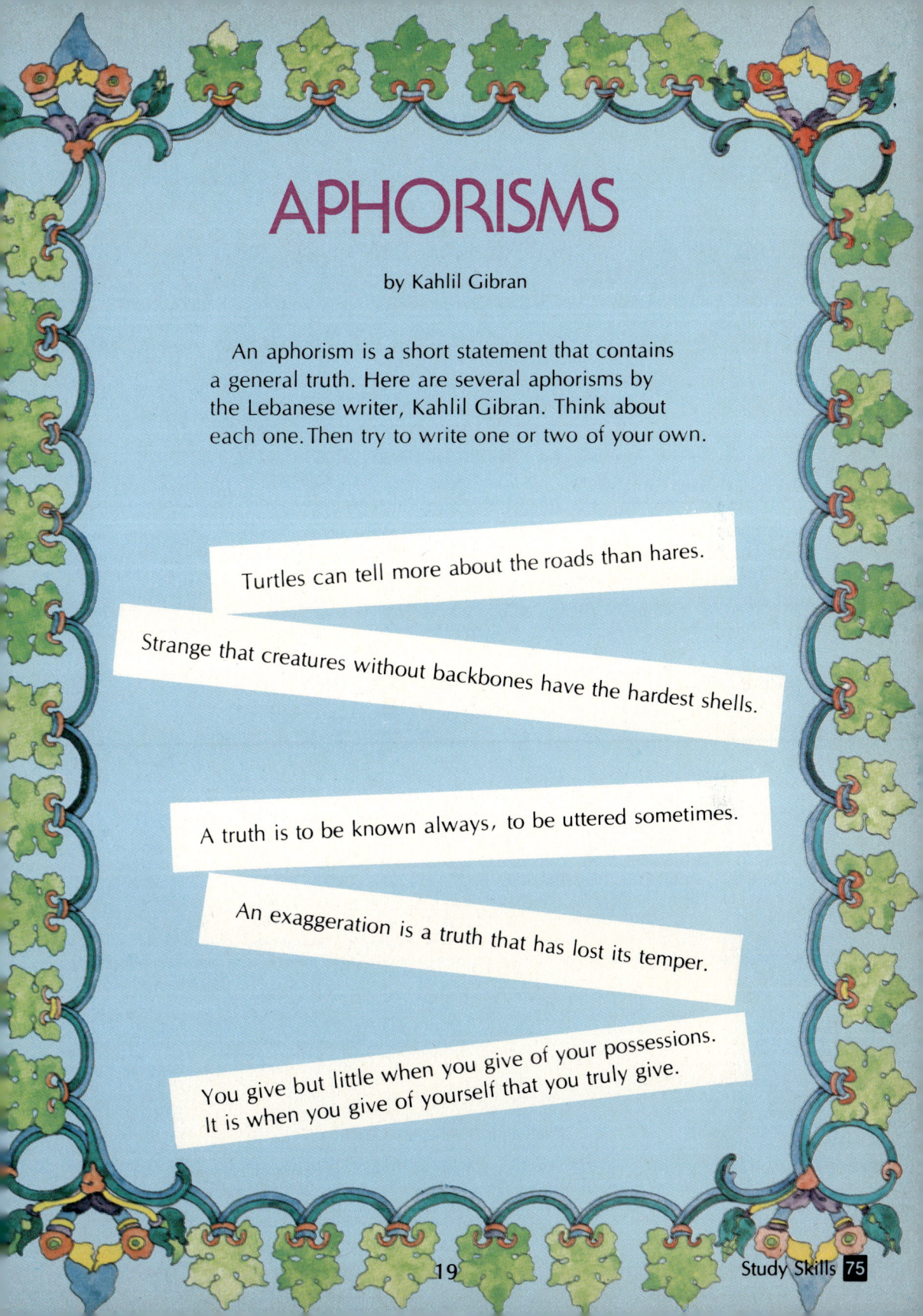

APHORISMS

by Kahlil Gibran

An aphorism is a short statement that contains a general truth. Here are several aphorisms by the Lebanese writer, Kahlil Gibran. Think about each one. Then try to write one or two of your own.

Turtles can tell more about the roads than hares.

Strange that creatures without backbones have the hardest shells.

A truth is to be known always, to be uttered sometimes.

An exaggeration is a truth that has lost its temper.

You give but little when you give of your possessions. It is when you give of yourself that you truly give.

Study Skills

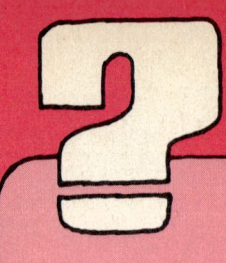

APHORISMS
(page 19)

1. Which of Gibran's aphorisms seems to say, there is a right and wrong time to tell what you think is true?

2. Choose the aphorism that means: Speed isn't everything; if you go too fast, you might not notice some important things.

3. Pick the aphorism that means: Sometimes people who put up a brave, noisy front are hiding the fact that they aren't sure or don't know what to do.

4. Choose the definition of the word *uttered*, as used in the aphorism on page 19.

    ut·ter[1] (ut/ər), *v.* **1.** to speak or pronounce. **2.** to give forth (a sound): *She uttered a groan.* [from the Middle English word *outre* "to pronounce, emit"]
    ut·ter[2] (ut/ər), *adj.* complete; total: *utter darkness;*

5. Choose the definition of *temper*, as used in, "An exaggeration is a truth that has lost its temper."

    tem·per (tem/pər), *n.* **1.** heat of mind or passion, shown in outbursts of anger: *He has quite a temper.* **2.** calm mood or state of mind: *to lose one's temper.* **3.** the degree of hardness given to a metal. —*v.* **4.** to soften or moderate: *to temper justice with mercy.*

ANSWERS

1. "A truth is to be known always, to be uttered sometimes."
2. "Turtles can tell more about the roads than hares."
3. "Strange that creatures without backbones have the hardest shells."
4. to speak or pronounce
5. calm mood or state of mind

EMERGENCY!

by Nick Pease

One bone-chilling, cold night, when even the air seemed brittle, the urgent whine of a siren cut through the stillness like a jagged blade. "Oooo-eeee, oooo-eeee, oooo-eeee," wailed the ambulance as it lurched and charged along the deserted streets toward the hospital. On a stretcher, in back, lay twelve-year-old Linda Wing, a victim of an auto accident. Just a few minutes before, her father had been bringing the family home from a weekend skiing trip, when a truck backed out suddenly from an alley. The wreckage told the rest of the story.

When the ambulance stopped at the emergency entrance of the hospital, the attendant sitting beside Linda glanced nervously out the rear window. To his relief, a police car with Linda's father and mother pulled in behind the ambulance. That meant they were all right. But Linda?

Linda's stretcher was rolled down the hall to the x-ray room. She didn't feel any pain, but she was scared. Then she saw Mike Berger, an x-ray technician. He had one of the most important jobs in the hospital. Without him, even the best surgeon might not know where to begin treatment. When he saw the scared expression in Linda's eye's, Mike started talking to her as he moved the heavy machinery into position.

"Hi," he said, "my name's Mike Berger. What's yours?"

"Linda," she said weakly. "Linda Wing."

"Well," he said, "looks like you've had a little accident. I'm an x-ray technician, and I'm going to take a few pictures now. Have you had x-rays before?"

"Yes, the dentist took x-rays of my teeth," Linda said.

"Good. Then you know it doesn't hurt. It's just like having your photograph taken, except you don't have to smile or say 'cheese.'"

Linda did smile then, a little smile.

"Do you feel any pain anywhere?" he asked.

"Mostly I just feel numb," said Linda, "except when I move my shoulder." She winced.

"Well, you don't have to move," Mike said gently. "You just take it easy, and I'll do all the work." When Mike looked up, he saw Linda's parents entering the laboratory. "Hey, Linda, I think you have some visitors already. You must be pretty popular."

Mike liked working with people. Any trained technician could set up the equipment and snap a picture, but it took a special talent to put patients at ease so a clear x-ray could be taken. And both doctors and patients knew that Mike was very good at his work.

Mike never thought about any other jobs he could have as an x-ray technician. He could probably make more money working in an airplane factory, x-raying pieces of metal for signs of weakness, but that wasn't for him.

He wheeled the stretcher to the x-ray table and lined up a photographic plate under Linda's shoulder. When everything was set up, Linda's parents left the room and Mike began x-raying. Carefully he lined up the x-ray machine for each shot, slipping in a new photographic plate and removing the old one. Then, reminding Linda to stay "as still as a statue," he stepped behind a radiation-proof lead door and took the shot. Each one took less than a second. Linda was beginning to enjoy all this special attention, and she had lots of questions.

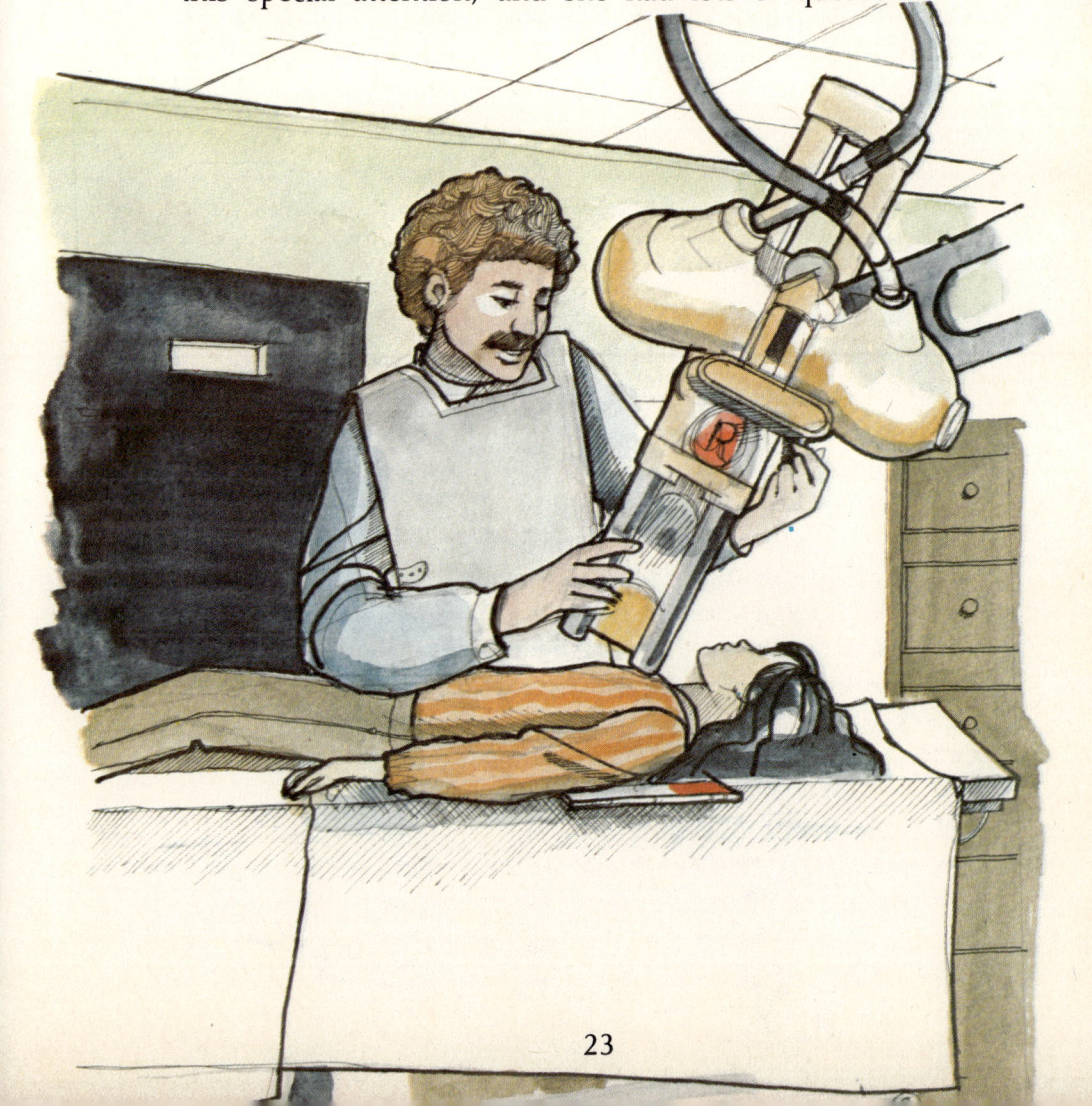

"How does all this work?"

"It's very simple, really," said Mike. "The x-ray machine sends out a beam of invisible rays that pass through your body. When the rays reach something solid, such as bone, they leave a shadow on the photographic plate below. The film on the plate is developed just like any ordinary film, and the negative that comes out is your x-ray. It's fast, too. Each one of these will take only about a minute and a half to develop."

"Wow! At our drugstore it takes a week and a half to get my pictures back," laughed Linda. "But why do you hide behind that door while the machine's on?"

"Just to be on the safe side," said Mike. "As you probably know, too much radiation can be dangerous. The patients don't have to worry, because the machine shuts itself off automatically. But the technicians who are exposed to it every day have to be careful of radiation build-up. So we stand behind that shield or wear a lead-lined apron when we work. And we all wear a little badge like this which shows how much radiation we've had. These are checked every month to be sure there's no danger."

"Are my x-rays ready yet?" asked Linda. She rubbed her right shoulder. "It hurts—do you think it's serious?"

"Your x-rays are ready," said Mike, "but I can't give you a diagnosis. I don't read the x-rays. That's the job of a specially trained person called a radiologist, who advises the doctor on what the pictures mean. Yours are on their way to Radiology right now, and soon you'll be seeing a doctor."

Linda gave him a scared look. "Will he give me shots?" she asked.

Mike folded his arms. "Well, Dr. Wing," he said, pretending to be stern, "my professional opinion is this: you won't change anything by worrying about it. And the truth is," he added, as he opened the door for Linda's parents, "I don't know."

A doctor, who was a staff member of the hospital, came in with Mr. and Mrs. Wing. The doctor performed routine tests to see that Linda's heart, blood pressure and other body functions were normal. While the doctor worked, Mike told Linda more about being an x-ray technician.

During his two-year hospital training, Mike had gained some valuable experience working nights on the job. "It is important to handle patients personally," he said, "because no two patients are exactly the same, and no book can tell you how to handle each problem."

Many of the night cases were accident victims, so he had learned to take sharp, accurate x-rays on the first try. In an emergency, that's vital. Those x-rays were mostly for broken bones. By day, Mike had learned how to use special dyes to photograph the bloodstream and internal organs, and often he also brought portable equipment into the operating room to assist during surgery.

X-ray technicians earn about the same salary as nurses, but many, like Mike, earn more by being "on call"—coming in at night to handle emergencies. Linda didn't say so, but she was glad Mike was on call that night.

Soon another doctor came in carrying the radiologist's report. It was good news—no breaks, sprains, or dislocations. Just a bruise on the shoulder. After all the excitement, however, Linda couldn't help feeling just a little disappointed. "I thought it would turn out to be something really serious," she said.

"I did, too," added Mike. "I was hoping this emergency would make me famous. You never know. It might have led to a TV series based on my career: Mike Berger—Crack Technologist!"

Everyone groaned, and Mike laughed.

"Well, it was nice meeting you anyway, Linda," Mike went on, "and I hope to see you again sometime. But if I do, please don't let it be at night, and *please* don't come through the emergency entrance!"

"I promise I won't," laughed Linda.

EMERGENCY!

(pages 21-26)

1. Why does an x-ray technician play an important role in the hospital?

2. What made the sound that "cut through the stillness like a jagged blade"? What else makes such a sound?

3. Why doesn't Mike work in a factory where he could make more money?

4. What happens when the x-rays passing through your body hit something solid, such as bone?

5. Find the word *technician* in the dictionary. Which syllable is stressed?

6. Look up *emergency* in the dictionary. Which syllable contains the *schwa* sound?

ANSWERS

1. Doctors need accurate x-rays to show them just where a patient's problem is.
2. It was an ambulance siren. It could also have been a police car or fire truck siren.
3. Mike likes working with people.
4. The bones leave a shadow on the photographic plate.
5. the second syllable
6. the third syllable

27

VAMPIRE BATS

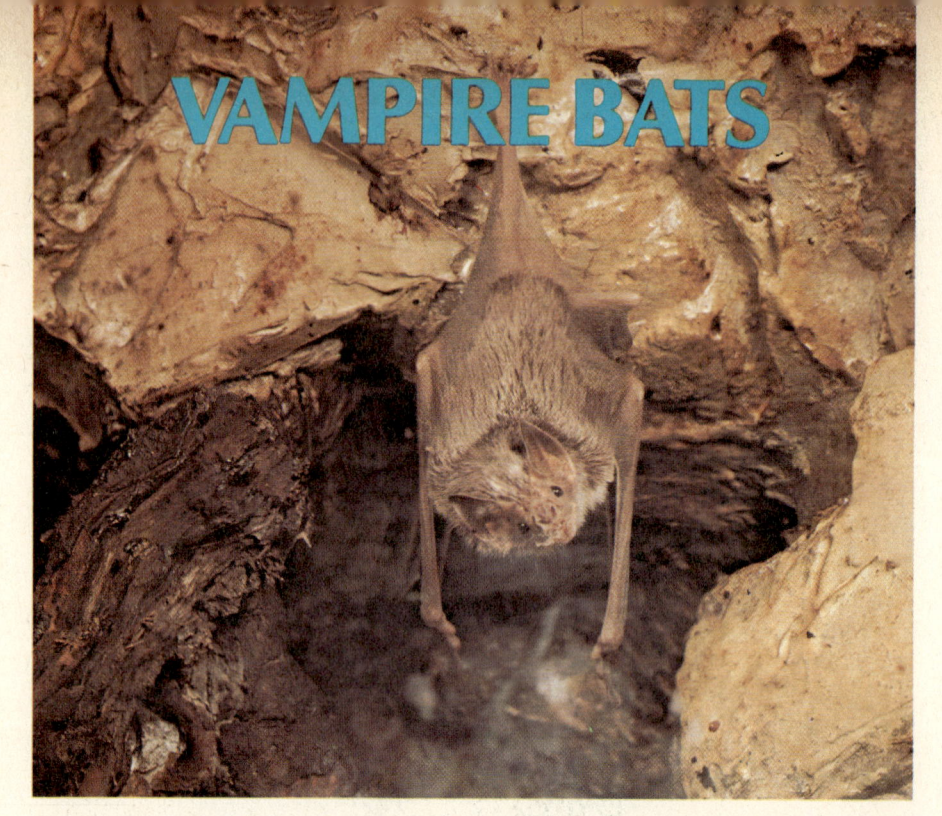

from *Bats—Wings in the Night*
by Patricia Lauber

Long ago the people of Slavic countries believed in blood-sucking ghosts. They called these ghosts "vampires." At night, they said, vampires rose from the grave and sucked the blood of living persons.

There was no such thing as a blood-sucking ghost. But early explorers of the Americas discovered living creatures that came out at night to feed upon the blood of animals. These creatures were bats, and so they came to be called vampire bats.

Vampires are New World bats. They live in Central and South America, from Argentina north to Mexico. They are found no place else in the world.

Scientists know of three kinds of vampire bat. The best known is *Desmodus rotundus*. It is a medium-sized bat with a round body and a fifteen-inch wingspread. *Desmodus* has very long thumbs and a soft pad at each wrist. It rests on these pads while feeding. It has a flat face with a pushed-in nose, something like that of a bulldog. The nose allows the bat to nuzzle close to its victim and slash the skin with its razor-sharp teeth.

Vampires like to live in very dark places. They are mostly found deep in caves, but they also live in mines, old wells, and hollow trees. They may live alone, in small groups, or in colonies of thousands. They share their shelter with other kinds of bat. In most cases, the vampires do not attack these bats.

Like many other bats, vampires hang by their feet when roosting. Unlike most other bats, they are nimble on all fours. They can walk quickly, dodge away from a net, and even bounce like rubber balls.

Vampires leave their shelter to feed only after dark. (The young stay behind in the roost.) *Desmodus* flies about three feet above the ground with slow, silent strokes. It will attack any quiet, warm-blooded animal. But its usual victims are horses, burros and cattle. *Desmodus* may land near a victim and walk up to it. Or the bat may land on the victim. A vampire weighs only about two ounces, and it lands so gently that the sleeping victim seldom wakes. The bat walks lightly over the victim, searching for a spot where there is little or no hair. There it shaves off a thin slice of skin.

Blood wells up from the small cut. The vampire puts its tongue to the wound. The sides of the tongue are turned down, so that the tongue forms a tube. It fits in a groove in the lower lip. The tongue moves back and forth in short strokes. Blood flows beneath the tongue into the mouth. A chemical in the bat's saliva keeps the blood from clotting.

The vampire drinks its fill, which is about an ounce of blood. Then it leaves, as gently and silently as it came. It flies off and hangs up to digest its meal.

The vampire takes only a small amount of blood. The loss of blood is not dangerous. The danger is that the vampires may carry diseases. They spread these diseases through their bites.

Then, too, in some places there are huge numbers of vampires. They are a threat to livestock in the area, for they return night after night to feed. Over a period of time they do great harm to the livestock. Where there are no livestock, vampires feed on wild animals, such as small mammals and birds.

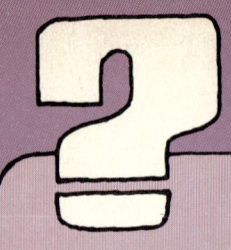

VAMPIRE BATS

(pages 28-29)

1. Where did the idea of a vampire originate?

2. What does the vampire bat do after it shaves off a thin slice of its victim's skin?

3. What are the bat's usual victims?

4. What is dangerous about the bite of the vampire bat?

5. Under which topic in an outline would you put this statement?
   Vampires like to live in very dark places.
   - Physical Characteristics
   - Environment
   - Activities

6. Choose the topic that would come first in an outline of this story.
   - Places Where Vampire Bats Are Found
   - Method by Which Vampire Bats Suck Blood

ANSWERS

1. in Slavic countries.
2. The bat puts its tongue to the wound and sucks its victim's blood.
3. horses, burros, cattle
4. If the bat is carrying a disease, it spreads the disease through its bite.
5. Environment
6. Places Where Vampire Bats Are Found

WONDERING WHY

from *Panther's Moon*
by Ruskin Bond

Bisnu, a twelve-year-old boy from the Himalaya Mountains of India, mourns for Sheroo, his beloved dog, who was killed by a panther. This chapter describes a second brush with death that leaves Bisnu and all of us wondering why.

Bisnu was not a very sentimental boy, but he sorrowed for his dog. He did not sleep that night, but turned restlessly from side to side, moaning softly.

Next morning when he went down to the stream to bathe, he missed the presence of his dog. He did not stay long in the water. It wasn't so much fun when there was no Sheroo to watch him.

When Bisnu's mother gave him his food, she told him to be careful and to hurry home that evening. A panther, even if it is only a lifter of sheep or dogs, is not to be trifled with. And this particular panther had shown some daring by seizing the dog even before it was dark. There was no question of staying away from school. If Bisnu remained at home every time a panther put in an appearance, he might just as well stop going to school altogether.

He set off even earlier than usual and reached the meeting of the paths long before Sarru. He did not wait for his friend because he did not feel like talking about the loss of his dog. It was not the day for the postman, so

Bisnu reached Kemptee without meeting anyone on the way. He tried to slip past the hospital gate unnoticed, but Dr. Taylor saw him, and the first thing she said was, "Where's Sheroo? I've got something for him."

When Dr. Taylor saw the boy's face, she knew at once something was wrong.

"What is it, Bisnu?" she asked. She looked quickly up and down the road. "Is it Sheroo?"

He nodded gravely. "A panther took him," he said.

"In the village?"

"No, while we were walking home through the forest. I did not see anything, but I heard."

Dr. Taylor knew that there was nothing she could say that would console him, and she tried to conceal the bone which she had brought out for the dog. But Bisnu noticed her hiding it behind her back, and the tears welled up in his eyes. He turned away and began running down the road.

His schoolmates noticed Sheroo's absence and questioned Bisnu. He had to tell them everything. They were full of sympathy, but they were also excited at what had happened, and kept pestering Bisnu for all the details. There was a lot of noise in the classroom, and Mr. Nautiyal had to call for order. When he learned what had happened, he patted Bisnu on the head and told him that he need not attend school for the rest of the day. But Bisnu did not want to go home. After school, he got into a fight with one of the boys, and that helped him forget.

Walking home through the scrub of the hillside, Bisnu saw a big brown owl get up and groggily but silently flap away. He was watching it idly when he became conscious of an unusual sound, rather like the twang of a telegraph wire when struck by a stone. Looking up, he was astonished to see a hawk swooping at the owl. With wings partly shut, it was coming down at a slant and at great speed.

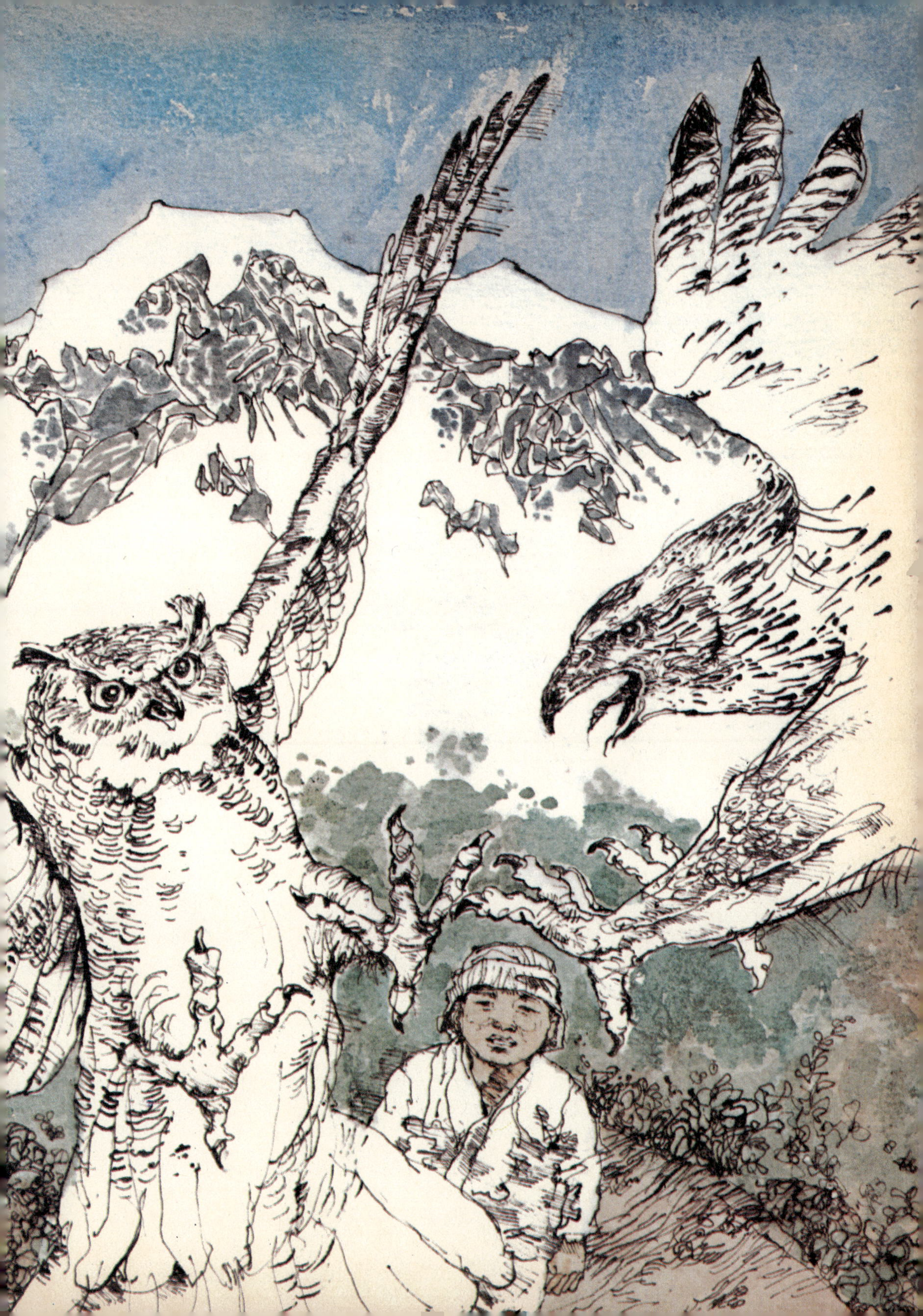

It was impossible for Bisnu to make out exactly what happened next. But it seemed as if the owl, without so much as a pause in its flight, turned quickly over and met the hawk beak to beak and claw to claw. The combatants met with a scream and a dull thud. With another thud they hit the ground some twenty feet below, disappearing momentarily from view.

Bisnu ran forward to see what was happening, but before he reached the spot the birds appeared again, locked together in a fierce embrace. The hawk, though much the smaller, was on top, trying hard to carry the owl, whose great brown wings were thrashing terribly. In silence, but for the thudding of the wings, they moved slowly away from Bisnu, swaying and reeling through the air in a cloud of feathers. The hawk was slowly but surely lifting the owl.

For fifty yards they staggered along, fighting furiously, and then the fight reached its frenzied climax. The beating of the brown wings redoubled; the hawk screamed shrilly. Then, turning over and over, they thudded to the ground again.

When Bisnu reached them, they were still locked together. Both birds were dead. It appeared from the wounds that the owl had gotten its head well in under the hawk first, and all the hawk could do was to stoop over and tear at its back.

For the rest of his walk home, Bisnu kept wondering why the hawk had attacked a bird as big and as strong as itself. Did the hawk know what it was attacking, or did it mistake the owl for some other bird? Perhaps it was confused by seeing the owl in daylight. Or perhaps it knew what it was attacking, and went through with it because of a hard-pressed family at home, or simply because it was hungry itself.

It had been a hungry panther that had taken Sheroo.

WONDERING WHY

(pages 31-34)

1. Look up *sentimental* in the dictionary. What was the author saying when he wrote, "Bisnu was not a very sentimental boy"?

2. Why did Bisnu feel better after he fought with one of the boys?

3. Why didn't Bisnu want to meet his best friends?

4. What did Bisnu wonder about when he found both the hawk and its victim dead?

5. Name the first place in the selection where you find out that Sheroo was killed by a panther.

6. Read the introduction to the story. How old is Bisnu, and where does he live?

ANSWERS

1. Bisnu was not an overly emotional person.
2. The fight helped him to forget the death of his dog.
3. He didn't feel like talking about the death of his dog.
4. He wondered whether the hawk had attacked the big, strong owl by mistake, or because it needed food.
5. the introduction
6. Bisnu is twelve, and he lives in the Himalaya Mountains of India.

. . . a time to plant

To Every Thing There Is a Season

Here's a poem from the most famous and widely read book of all time. Do you know which book this passage comes from?

To every thing there is a season and a time to every purpose under the heaven.

A time to be born, and a time to die: a time to plant, and a time to pluck up that which is planted:

A time to kill, and a time to heal: a time to break down, and a time to build up:

. . . and a time to pluck up that which is planted

    A time to weep, and a time to laugh: a time to mourn and a time to dance:
    A time to cast away stones, and a time to gather stones together: a time to embrace, and a time to refrain from embracing:
    A time to get, and a time to lose: a time to keep, and a time to cast away:
    A time to rend, and a time to sew: a time to keep silence, and a time to speak:
    A time to love, and a time to hate: a time of war, and a time of peace.

    This poem comes from Chapter 3 of Ecclesiastes, in the Bible.

To Every Thing There Is a Season

(pages 36-37)

1. There are appropriate times to do different things. Name some of the different times mentioned in this poem.

2. Look up *rend* in the dictionary. What does "a time to rend" mean?

3. What is the message of this biblical poem?

4. What time follows the planting time?

5. In what part of a book would you find the names of reference books used by an author?

6. In what part of a social science book would you find the definition of the word *season*?

ANSWERS

1. Some of these times are: a time to be born, a time to die, a time to love, a time to hate, a time to embrace, etc.
2. It is a time to tear things apart, to split or divide them.
3. Many things we do are the opposites of each other; yet, there is a proper time for doing each of them.
4. Harvest time follows the planting time.
5. the bibliography
6. the glossary

Dear March, Come In!

by Emily Dickinson

For the poet Emily Dickinson, Time and Nature were very important and personal subjects. Here is a poem she wrote about the month of March.

Dear March—Come in—
How glad I am—
I hoped for you before—

Put down your Hat—
You must have walked—
How out of Breath you are—
Dear March, how are you, and the Rest—
Did you leave Nature well—
Oh March, Come right up stairs with me—
I have so much to tell—

I got your Letter, and the Birds—
The Maples never knew that you were coming—till I called
I declare—how Red their Faces grew—
But, March, forgive me—and
All those Hills you left for me to Hue—
There was no Purple suitable—
You took it all with you—

Who knocks? That April.
Lock the Door—
I will not be pursued—
He stayed away a Year to call
When I am occupied—
But trifles look so trivial
As soon as you have come

That Blame is just as dear as Praise
And Praise as mere as Blame—

Dear March, Come In!

(page 39)

1. What does *Hue* mean? Was *Hue* used as a noun or verb in this poem?

2. When a month is given human characteristics, what do you call this poetic device?

3. Is the poet looking forward to meeting April? How do you know?

4. The poet writes about March as if it were _____.
   - a welcome guest
   - an unwanted visitor
   - an intruder
   - an embarrassed maple

5. What two themes are important in Emily Dickinson's poetry?

6. In a science book, a section on the maples might appear in the chapter entitled _____.
   Our Solar System   A Forest Walk   Aquatic Wonders

ANSWERS

1. Hue means color. It was used as a verb here, but it is normally a noun.
2. personification
3. No. In the fourth stanza, when April knocks, the poet wants to lock the door.
4. a welcome guest
5. Time and Nature
6. A Forest Walk

AUGUSTE, THE MIME

from *Burnish Me Bright* by Julia Cunningham

Poor Auguste! He could not speak. This lonely, mistreated orphan worked as a farm hand for Madame Fer. His only friend had been Monsieur Hilaire, once France's greatest mime. He taught Auguste the great art of mime. This story tells how Auguste, more lonely than ever after Hilaire's death, uses his new talent to help Avril Cresson, the little village girl who lies ill.

The sun was still red and rising. Auguste, in the far pasture with the cows, heard his name, small and shrieked. It was still an hour to breakfast and Madame Fer never varied her routine so as not to lose a moment of Auguste's work time. He made a running jump over the one calf, pretending to be a cowbird, and then fell into a trot toward the house.

She was poised in the doorway, her arms crossed. "I called you twice!"

He waited, his eyes on her shoes, for the usual lengthy tirade.

Instead she spoke to someone behind her. "See what I mean? His silence is impertinent! And I am certain that what he is thinking would crisp an angel. Well? Come in and eat!"

As he entered the bare room he saw Madame Cresson seated by the fire, her coat still on, her cheeks pink as though she had hurried. "Perhaps she'll improve before the day's end."

"One hopes so," said Madame Fer gloomily. "But the child has always been fragile."

"Yes, Avril is like a butterfly, my husband always says," said the mother, "and perhaps she is destined only for a brief life." She took out her handkerchief.

The farm woman patted her clumsily on the back. "Trouble is you've been alone with this responsibility too long. Company's what you need during the watch." She coiled a fat brown shawl over her shoulders. She swept the bowl from the table and placed it in the sink, then thrust a heal of bread at Auguste. "If I'm very late getting back, you just feed yourself." She propelled Madame Cresson and Auguste outdoors and secured the lock. She did not glance at the boy again but led the way down the road, the other woman three steps behind and pushing herself to keep up.

For the next few hours Auguste worked at high speed in order to extend his freedom at the end of the day. But when he sat down at ease against a fencepost near the front gate to eat his bread he saw, almost within reach, a green and blue spotted butterfly. It alighted on a stem of milkweed. Its wings fluttered for an instant, then stilled. Auguste stopped chewing. A kind of immense pause descended over the meadow as though a signal had been received by every beetle and bird and stir of air. Then, as though possessed of an inner whirlwind, the butterfly revived, shot into space and then, wildly faltering, its wings now a shudder of colors, dropped to the ground.

Auguste felt himself held by the tiny death. His hands trembled a little. He stuffed the bread into his jacket pocket and very slowly touched his palms together and watched them become wings. They were remembering the drama. At last they ceased. Auguste wiped the perspiration from his forehead and the words of the woman came back to him. "Avril is like a butterfly." He took a deep breath and got up. If she were dying as Monsieur Hilaire had died then she would be going to the same place, to the same blurred landscape of light and music and bright wings. Maybe she would take a message. For the first time since his teacher's absence he felt joy, and without hesitating strode down the highroad.

Auguste knew that he must not be seen. Any one of the village people would report his coming to Madame Fer, and for punishment she might lock him up in the barn. This had happened once when he was six.

He remembered where Avril lived. In the days when he had gone to school he had noticed where she turned in. The house was the largest, next to the Mayor's, two-storied, and constructed of wood instead of plaster. An oak tree shaded one side of it. Auguste entered the village by the alleys, and as fast as he could, clambered up into the concealment of the oak branches. Settling down, he looked and listened.

Madame Cresson was speaking. "She's in a bad way. Won't eat, can't seem to sleep peacefully, thrashes around all night. I don't know. I just don't know."

Another woman spoke. It was Madame Fer. "No fever, you say?"

"Not this time. Just fades off, wispy-like. My husband and I can almost clock it. She gets very tired and pale as chalk. Then stops wanting to eat. Then takes to bed. Happened ever since she was a baby."

Then the mother's voice came from the open window immediately opposite his perch. It was almost whispered. "See how she lies? Avril? *Cherie?* Are you awake?"

A sound like a small owl in a chimney replied, "Yes, Maman."

"Madame Fer is here to see you. Will you try a cup of soup now?"

"No, thank you. Later, Maman."

"We'll leave you then, but remember your promise to eat."

Auguste heard the bedroom door shut, then the hushed chatter of the two women returning to the ground floor.

He lowered his body, hands around the branch, and swung himself back and forth three times. On the third swing his feet found the wide window sill and he let the motion carry him upward and against the window. For a second he stayed, flat as a silhouette, against the glass. But the girl in the bed had her head turned away. He angled himself inside and went to stand at the foot of her bed. The green, flower-sprigged coverlet accentuated her pallor. Her hair that reminded Auguste of autumn sunlight was tousled upon the pillow. The whole image had an underwater feeling and the boy recalled all the hours he had spent on his stomach, his nose touching the surface of the stream, regarding the world below, himself a fish.

But with a soft suddenness it changed. Avril opened her eyes. Such a blue shone from the pallor of her face, it was the sapphire of Monsieur Hilaire come to life. Two of them.

"Who are you?" There was no fright in her tone, only a kind of submerged wonderment.

Auguste bowed as though making an entrance. He would become her court juggler, for surely this was a queen. From his pockets he drew forth five imaginary balls. One after the other they took to the air, circling each other faster and faster. Auguste's hands never faltered in their rhythm. Then, both arms outflung, he consigned them to vanishment and plucked from nowhere two hoops. First he whirled them on both arms, then jumped into them and twirled them on one leg, dancing on the other. These, too, were discarded. Last he squatted on the floor, his legs and arms folded tight around him. Avril could only see the top of his head. She sat up to watch. For a moment he remained enclosed. What was he? A seed? Then slowly, slowly he began to rise, to unfold until he stood upright and his hands were leaves and his head a flower. For five seconds he held the magic. Then relaxed into himself.

A clapping, a weak effort at applause, cued him into a low bow. And when he faced the girl again he was smiling.

"Oh! Oh!" was all she could seem to say. Then a smile as real as the color of her eyes covered her face and her cheeks pinked. "I do know you! I do! You're Auguste, the boy who can't talk. Oh, that was—that was like a fairy tale! Thank you!"

Auguste turned to leave. Soon now her mother would be coming back.

"Don't go! Please!"

He shook his head, but as he put one leg over the window sill he gestured first to her and then to himself and Avril knew what he meant. She must find him. She nodded. "I will, just as soon as I can."

He placed his forefinger to his mouth.

"I know. I mustn't tell."

She watched him fling himself onto the nearest branch and then the leaves covered him. And when her mother came next to observe her the woman cried out, "But what has happened, *cherie*? You are sitting up! Madame Fer, come look! There has been a miracle!"

Avril merely smiled. "*Maman*, could I have that soup now? And maybe a piece of toast?"

AUGUSTE, THE MIME

(pages 41-45)

1. What do Auguste's hands remember as they become wings?

2. When Auguste remembers that "Avril is like a butterfly," he feels joy. Why?

3. What part of Avril's face does the following passage describe?
   > Such a blue shone from the pallor of her face, it was the sapphire of Monsieur Hilaire come to life. Two of them.

4. Name three things Auguste does to entertain Avril.

5. Choose the letter for the words missing from this sentence.
   Auguste's teacher was named _____.
   A. Madame Fer   B. Monsieur Cresson
   C. Monsieur Hilaire

6. After Auguste entertained Avril, the girl _____.
   A. went to sleep   B. felt better   C. cried

ANSWERS

1. the delicate butterfly's death
2. She is as delicate as the butterfly and she may die as it did. He believes he can give her a message to take to his dear teacher, M. Hilaire, who has just died.
3. This passage describes Avril's eyes.
4. Auguste mimes the juggling of balls, the twirling of hoops, and the growth of a seed into a flower.
5. C
6. B

FACES

from *Collected Shorter Poems*
and *Thank You, Fog*
by W.H. Auden

The poet W.H. Auden often used his wit
to point out the quirks of human relationships.

I'm beginning to lose patience
With my personal relations:
They are not deep,
And they are not cheap.

Private faces in public places
Are wiser and nicer
Than public faces in private places.

Bound to ourselves for life,
we must learn how to
put up with each other.

The Champion smiles—What Personality!
The Challenger scowls—How horrid he must be!
But let the Belt change hands and they change places,
Still from the same old corners come the same grimaces.

FACES

(page 47)

1. What does the poet mean by saying his personal relations "are not deep and they are not cheap"?

2. Look up *grimace* in the dictionary. What are grimaces?

3. Which attitude does the author show in the third poem?
   - tolerance
   - intolerance

4. What sports use differently colored belts as awards?

5. How many cards would there be in the card catalog for the book, *Collected Shorter Poems* by W. H. Auden? What are the names of the cards?

6. What is the first thing you would see on the author card for the above book?

ANSWERS

1. The personal relations he is referring to do not mean very much to him, but they cost him a lot of time, effort, or money.
2. Grimaces are facial expressions in which the features are twisted in a way that shows pain or disgust.
3. tolerance
4. karate, jujitsu and judo
5. It would have three cards: subject card, author card, title card.
6. Auden, W. H.

CHINESE PARABLES

from *The Wisdom of China and India* Edited by Lin Yutang

A parable is a short story, told to teach a moral or ethical truth. Lin Yutang, who was a great Chinese writer, translated these ancient Chinese parables. The first parable is followed by an explanation of what the writer was trying to teach us. Can you explain the other parables?

THE BLIND MAN'S IDEA OF THE SUN

There was a man born blind. He had never seen the sun and asked about it of people who could see. Someone told him, "The sun's shape is like a brass tray." The blind man struck the brass tray and heard its sound. Later when he heard the sound of a bell, he thought it was the sun. Again someone told him, "The sunlight is like that of a candle," and the blind man felt the candle, and thought that was the sun's shape. Later he felt a big key and thought it was a sun. The sun is quite different from a bell or a key, but the blind man cannot tell their difference because he has never seen the sun. The truth is harder to see than the sun, and when people do not know it they are exactly like the blind man.

> From what is said of the brass tray, one imagines a bell, and from what is said about a candle, one imagines a key. In this way, one gets ever further and further away from the truth.

THE CRANE AND THE CLAM

Chao was going to invade Yen. Su Tai went to speak to King Huei of Chao on Yen's behalf. "This morning," said Su Tai, "when I was coming on my way, I was passing the Yi River. There I saw a clam sunning itself in the sun, and a crane came along to peck at its flesh, and the clam shut its shell on the crane's beak tightly. The crane said, 'If it doesn't rain today and doesn't rain tomorrow, there will be a dead clam.' And the clam also said, 'If you can't get out today and can't get out tomorrow, there will be a dead crane.' Neither of the two was willing to let go, when a fisherman came up and caught them both."

KING HUAN LOST HIS HAT

King Huan of Ch'i was drunk one day and lost his hat. For three days he shut himself up for shame, without giving audience. Kuan Chung said to the King, "This is disgrace for a ruler. Why don't you make amends by some generous act?" Accordingly, the King opened the granary and distributed grains to the poor for three days. The people praised the King for his generosity, and said, "Why does not he lose his hat again?"

THE OWL AND THE QUAIL

An owl met a quail, and the quail asked, "Where are you going?" "I am going east," was the owl's reply. "May I ask why?" then asked the quail. "The people of the village hate my screeching noise," replied the owl. "That is why I am going east." Then said the quail, "What you should do is change that screeching noise. If you can't, you will be hated for it even if you go east."

THE MAN WHO SAW ONLY GOLD

There was a man of Ch'i who desired to have gold. He dressed up properly and went out in early morning to the market. He went straight to the gold dealer's shop and snatched the gold away and walked off. The officers arrested him and questioned him: "Why, the people were all there. Why did you rob them of gold in broad daylight?" And the man replied, "I only saw the gold. I didn't see any people."

LOOKS LIKE A THIEF

There was a man who had lost money and thought that his neighbor's son had stolen it. He looked at him and it seemed his gait was that of a thief, his expression was that of a thief, and all his gestures and movements were like those of a thief. Soon afterwards he found the money in a bamboo drainpipe. Again he looked at the neighbor's son and neither his movements nor his gestures were those of a thief.

MEASUREMENTS FOR SHOES

A certain man of Cheng was going to buy himself a new pair of shoes. First he took measurements of his feet, and left them in his seat. These he forgot to bring along when he went to the streets, and after entering a shoe shop, he said to himself, "Oh, I have forgotten to bring along the measurements and must go back to bring them." So he did. But when he returned, the shop was closed already and he failed to buy any shoes. Someone said to him, "Why didn't you let them try the shoes on your feet?" And the man replied, "I would rather trust the measurements than trust myself."

CHINESE PARABLES

(pages 49-52)

1. Name the parable which teaches you that moving away will not solve your problems; they go with you.

2. Name the parable which shows that a person's greed can blind that person to everything else.

3. In "The Crane and the Clam," what happened after the clam shut its shell on the crane's beak?

4. In "King Yuan Lost His Hat," the people thought the king gave them grain because he lost his hat. What was the real reason?

5. How would you locate information on Chinese history in an encyclopedia?

6. How would you locate information about Lin Yutang in an encyclopedia?

ANSWERS

1. "The Owl and the Quail"
2. "The Man Who Saw Only Gold"
3. Neither creature was willing to let go, and a fisherman came and caught them both.
4. He was told he should make up for neglecting his duties. He had been hiding because he was ashamed of having drunk too much.
5. Look for the C volume. In an entry on China, there is a section on Chinese history.
6. Look under Lin Yutang in the L volume.

ANIMAL CRACKERS

Poems from *The Selected Verse of Odgen Nash*

An Introduction to Dogs

The dog is man's best friend.
He has a tail on one end.
Up in front he has teeth.
And four legs underneath.

Dogs like to bark.
They like it best after dark.
They not only frighten prowlers away
But also hold the sandman at bay.

A dog that is indoors
To be let out implores.
You let him out and what then?
He wants back in again.

Dogs display reluctance and wrath
If you try to give them a bath.
They bury bones in hideaways
And half the time they trot sideways.

They cheer up people who are frowning,
And rescue people who are drowning,
They also track mud on beds,
And chew people's clothes to shreds.

Dogs in the country have fun.
They run and run and run.
But in the city this species
Is dragged around on leashes.

Dogs are upright as a steeple
And much more loyal than people.
Well people may be reprehensibler
But that's probably because they are sensibler.

The Rhinoceros

The rhino is a homely beast,
For human eyes he's not a feast.
Farewell, farewell, you old rhinoceros,
I'll stare at something less prepoceros.

The Camel

The camel has a single hump;
The dromedary, two;
Or else the other way around.
I'm never sure. Are you?

The Duck

Behold the duck.
It does not cluck.
A cluck it lacks.
It quacks.
It is specially fond
Of a puddle or pond.
When it dines or sups,
It bottoms ups.

ANIMAL CRACKERS

(pages 54-55)

1. What does the author mean when he says that dogs "hold the sandman at bay"?

2. Look up *reluctance* and *wrath* in the dictionary. According to Ogden Nash, how does a dog act if you try to give it a bath?

3. What real phrases do *reprehensibler* and *sensibler* stand for?

4. The word *prepoceros* in *The Rhinoceros* is a variation of what real word? What does the real word mean?

5. You might want to ride a camel across the Sahara Desert someday. In what reference book would you find the exact location of the Sahara Desert?

6. Suppose ducks could read. In what book would they find the times of high and low tides?

ANSWERS

1. A dog's bark can keep you awake at night.
2. A dog acts unwilling and angry if you try to bathe it.
3. *Reprehensibler* stands for more reprehensible. *Sensibler* stands for more sensible.
4. *Preposterous* is the real word, which means completely contrary to reason, absurd, foolish.
5. an atlas
6. an almanac

OBSESSION

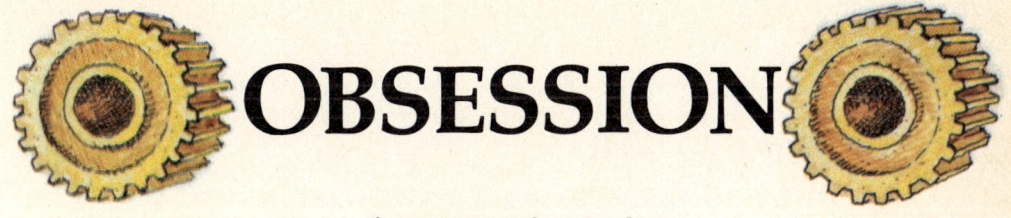

from *A Time for Watching*
by Gunilla Norris

A ten-year-old Swedish boy, Joachim Magnuson, had one desire in life—to find out how things worked. A doll that said "Mama," a scale, radio, clock—any machine, no matter to whom it belonged—was fair game for Joachim's inquisitive hands, fingers, and eyes. Joachim had an *obsession* for taking things apart. Poor Joachim. He had gotten into so much trouble that his father decided to keep a watchful eye on him at the post office, where Mr. Magnuson was the postmaster.

The next morning at the breakfast table Joachim felt a bit strange and awkward. He did not look at his parents but slid into his painted chair silently. Then, as from a distance, he heard Papa say, "How about coming to the post office with me today, Joachim?"

Joachim looked up. "Fine," he said, trying to sound pleased and surprised at once. But it came out strangely.

"I could use a little help from my big boy," continued Papa. "We'll do some really good work."

Startled, Joachim looked at his father. Papa never talked like that. Joachim frowned.

"We'll be together the whole day," continued Papa, and Joachim saw him look at Mamma in an "Am I doing all right?" sort of way. Joachim glanced quickly at Mamma. She was smiling, and the smile said, "Thank you, Gustav," plain as day. Joachim suddenly felt awful.

Why did they act like that? It was all pretend. Papa needed help like he needed three sets of legs. Last night he had felt . . . not really sorry . . . but different. But now . . . Joachim bent forward over his oatmeal. He would have to go with Papa, he knew that. There was nothing else to do.

"Are you trying to eat your oatmeal with your nose?" asked Karin, and Greta laughed.

"Girls!" snapped Papa and stood up. "Come on, Joachim, let's go."

They went out the dutch door and down the gravel road. The daisies bobbed in the wind near the ditches, and a barn swallow flew by. They walked silently. Then Joachim saw Mr. Kjellgren coming toward them.

"Hello there, Magnuson!" said Mr. Kjellgren. "Going to keep close tabs on that son of yours today, I hope."

Papa laughed in an embarrassed way.

Joachim looked down at the gravel. His insides felt pinched and miserable. So that was what Papa had in mind—keeping close tabs so he would not have to be ashamed of him. Joachim bit his lip and closed his eyes while the men were talking. He could feel the early summer breeze across his face. He was not going to cry. He was not going to think about anything. He shut his eyes more tightly.

Then a vision of Gubben Janson's house sprang into his head. He imagined it whole and beautiful. In there were clocks and machines, wonderful constructions that couldn't care less about keeping tabs. That was the great thing Mamma and Papa didn't seem to know or care about. Machines never scolded or misunderstood or even felt. They whirred on comfortably in their ordered ways. And Joachim longed to be with them, longed to know their secret workings.

"Joachim! Let's go. There's lots of work to do."

Joachim drifted back to the gravel road, to Mr. Kjellgren, and to the morning ahead. He shivered, and then silently he moved behind his father into the little post office.

"Now then," said Papa, "let's see where we'll put you to work." He looked around and scratched his head. "Where can we settle you?" Papa frowned as his eyes darted around the room. Then Joachim's face grew stiff. Now he knew it had all been pretend. Suddenly he couldn't stand it anymore. His eyes flashed.

"You don't need help," he blurted out. "You're just trying to keep tabs on me like Mr. Kjellgren said."

"Joachim," said Papa, "that is no way to speak to your elders."

"You don't care," said Joachim, "as long as I'm not in trouble, as long as you don't have to be ashamed."

Papa looked hurt. "Whatever gave you that idea?"

"It's true!" cried Joachim.

"No, it's not true," said his father. "When you've calmed down, we'll talk about it. But right now there's no need for this conversation at all. Take the stool and sit at the back counter. I want you to weigh some letters."

"Of course, he didn't want to talk about it!" thought Joachim. Sullenly he drew the high stool over to the counter.

"Here's the scale," said Papa. "Here are the letters. Write the weight on the right hand corner of the envelopes."

Joachim was left alone. Slowly he climbed up on the stool and twisted his wiry legs around the rungs. He stared at the letters. He picked one up and flopped it onto the scale. The mechanism jiggled. Slowly Joachim forgot the world around him. He watched the scale even out. If he had a screwdriver, he could find out what the scale looked like inside, how it was made. Silently he slid off the stool. His father was deep in conversation with a customer at the window. Joachim scurried around the post office. At last he found an old letter opener. It could serve as a screwdriver.

Slowly, painstakingly, he took the scale apart. There lay

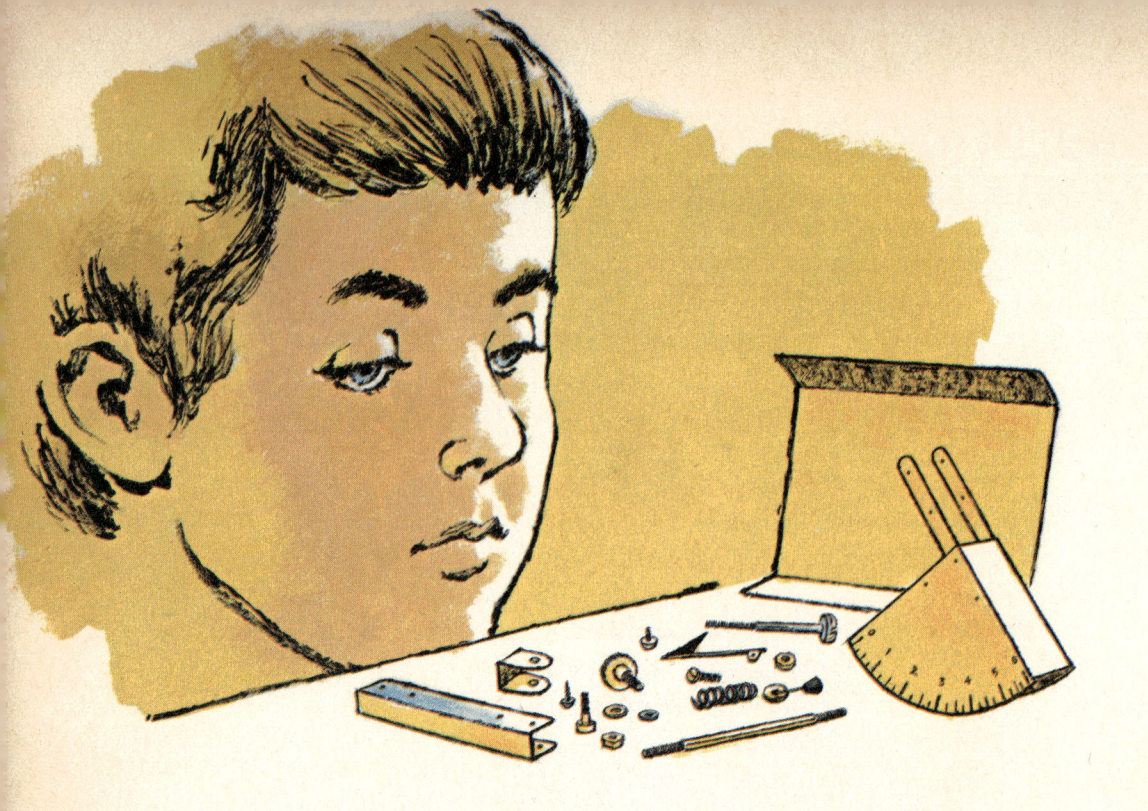

the vital parts all in order on the counter. To Joachim it was as though the world lay before him. There was the shaft, there were the balancing beam and the joint. He was so absorbed he didn't notice his father standing next to him.

"So," said Papa, "you have it apart. Now what?" Joachim looked up. Suddenly he felt uncertain.

"Now what?" asked his father again.

"I can put it together," mumbled Joachim.

"That's not the point," said Papa.

Joachim looked down. He wanted to pull his head into his shirt, as if a storm were about to break just above him. But nothing happened.

Papa went over to the post office window and shut it.

"All right, Joachim," he said. "Look at me."

Joachim looked up uneasily.

"First, I'm glad you have an interest in machines and how they work. That's fine. But," Papa looked at him sternly, "I want you to listen carefully. If you are told to weigh letters, then weigh letters. I need that scale right now. It has worked perfectly well for me. I have to get some packages off on the next mail car. I promised they would be on it."

"I'll have it together soon," said Joachim.

"But you had no right in the first place to take the scale apart without permission," said Papa.

"The packages can go with the next car," said Joachim defiantly.

"Yes, they can. But it means I've broken a promise just waiting for you to put that scale together."

"I was right," said Joachim. "You don't care about me. You don't care about how things work or anything." Somehow it didn't matter what he said. Joachim felt angry and empty.

"Listen, Joachim," said Papa. "Would I be cross if I didn't care about things? I care that the scale is all in pieces. I care that you disobeyed my instructions. I care what you do to other people."

Joachim looked at his scuffed shoes. What was the use? All Papa wanted was the mail scale to work and Joachim not to annoy anyone. He only cared about *not* being ashamed.

"Joachim," his father put a hand on his shoulder.

Joachim winced and looked away.

"I don't know everything in your head. You're probably feeling pretty misunderstood. But why don't you try to do some of your own understanding?"

Joachim knew he was expected to answer. All he wanted to do was to leave and bang the door.

"All right?" his father asked.

Joachim gave as small a nod as possible.

"That's good," sighed Papa. "Now let's see you put the scale together."

Slowly Joachim looked up at the counter. There was the scale spread out with its secret parts exposed. It was worth every bit of scolding. Those parts were beautiful. Joachim touched them gently.

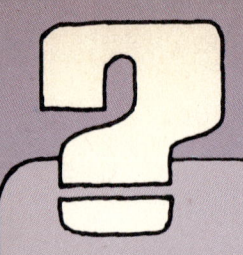

OBSESSION

(pages 57-61)

1. What is Joachim's feeling when he thinks, "Papa needed help like he needed three sets of legs"?

2. Why does Joachim find machines comforting?

3. How does Joachim upset his father after his father tells him to weigh the letters?

4. In the story, "Joachim twisted his wiry legs around the rungs of a stool." Is Joachim thin or fat? How can you tell?

5. This selection can best be described as _____.
   - autobiography
   - fiction
   - science fiction

6. Could this story be nonfiction? Why, or why not?

ANSWERS

1. Joachim feels badly that his father doesn't really need him. He also feels angry.
2. Machines don't care about keeping tabs on Joachim; they never scold or misunderstand.
3. Rather than weigh the letters on the scale, Joachim takes the scale apart.
4. Joachim is thin; his legs are described as "wiry."
5. fiction
6. Yes. It could have happened in real life.

62

TRILLIONS

a science fiction story from the book
by Nicholas Fisk

PART ONE

On a sunny but windy day in May, Harbortown and Harbortown alone received a heavy shower of Trillions.

There was no rain and no clouds. In the windy, open sky there was a slight darkening—a cloud patch that glittered in the sunlight. Then there was the sandstormy, rattling hiss as the Trillions came. Their showering lasted perhaps fifteen minutes. When it was over, there were drifts of Trillions everywhere. Trillions packed inches deep against a garden fence; Trillions glittering in drifts over roads and gardens; Trillions caught between the windows and window frames of houses and cars; Trillions edging the gutters, sparkling in the clefts of branches, lying thinly on the roofs of cars.

A few people were frightened by the Trillions. Most were puzzled and curious. The children were excited. "I've got millions. . .billions. . .Trillions!" they cried.

While the other children squeaked and jumped or sifted and sorted the Trillions, Bem collected a single jar full of them and walked down the road to Scott's house—and nearly collided with Scott, who was just leaving his house to visit Bem.

"Come inside, Bem," said Scott. "What do you make of it?"

Bem put a few Trillions on a glass slide, set up the microscope rapidly and peered into it.

"Two!" he said. "That's odd. You look."

"Two what?"

"Two sorts. See for yourself."

Scott put his eye to the microscope. What he saw amazed and dazzled him. It was as if he looked at priceless jewels, cut and faceted into superb circular gemstones. Under the microscope, the colors were even more startling than they were under normal light. He increased the magnification to concentrate on one particular Trillion. It looked like a great ruby. Then he shifted the slide to what appeared as a giant emerald, with a thousand geometrical faces cut in it.

"Do you notice? Two sorts?" said Bem.

Scott looked again, comparing one Trillion with another.

"You're right, Bem. Two sorts. Only two... One like a doughnut, with a hollow in the center—"

"Not a hollow, a complete hole," interrupted Bem.

"And the other with—"

"The other like a doughnut again, but with a spike sticking out of the center. I suppose it's the same on both sides?"

"Yes, the same both sides. Just the same. Like a jeweled doughnut with jeweled pyramids coming out of the center. You could spin it like a top."

"While the other sort has a hole in the center...do you notice something else?"

"What about?"

"About the edges. Look at the way the outside edges are cut."

Scott peered down the microscope, then lifted his head. "What do you mean about the edges? All I can see is a whole lot of regular triangular cuttings. The cuttings cover the whole of the outside of the doughnut shape—"

"Let me look for a moment," said Bem, butting his head against Scott so that Scott had to move. Bem fiddled with the needle as he looked, then said, "Have a look!"

Scott carefully put his eye to the microscope. Bem, he saw, had moved two Trillions together so that they touched. Although the Trillions were of different size, they "geared" together perfectly.

"They're like interlocking bricks—you know, those children's construction things!" said Scott.

"That's not all. They fit together edge to edge, but they also fit together on top of each other. You can see how the ones with pyramids in the middle could lock into the ones with doughnut holes. You could *build* with them!"

Scott was about to look through the microscope again, when Bem's sister Panda came rushing in, trampling over the sheets of paper on the floor and shaking the microscope.

"Watch out!" shouted Bem, too late.

"They're fantastic!" shouted Panda. "Oh, never mind the microscope—they're *marvelous*!" She went on, "I bet you don't know about them!"

"Know *what* about *what*?"

"About the Trillion things! They can do tricks! All on their own! Come and see!"

She squatted down on the stones of the patio, holding a piece of chalk. With this she made a simple squiggle—a rough "S." She scattered Trillions loosely over the "S," then she sat back on her heels, looking triumphant.

Very slowly, piece by piece, the Trillions began to move. Looking closely, you could see one Trillion nudge another—gear with it—turn it—move it!

Then more Trillions would combine to form a geared-together mass. The process would go faster now. Some Trillions would lock with more Trillions, and still more, until the whole collection would shift like sand.

At last, the Trillions finished their work. And now, replacing the "S" that Panda had made was another "S" made entirely of Trillions. An "S" correct in every detail, however tiny. Where Panda's finger had slipped slightly and made a jerky curve, the Trillions' curve was jerky too. Where the chalk was grainy, the Trillions' line was grainy.

Scott shook his head. "There's never been anything like this before. There just can't have been..."

Outside in the streets, there was a new commotion. The morning editions of the newspapers had arrived. As fast as the men and boys in the vans could unload, hands grabbed. The headline screamed—

TRILLIONS
World scientists probe invaders from space
Friend—or deadly foe?

PART TWO

The army was sent to Harbortown and tried to destroy the Trillions with traps, machines and nuclear weapons. But the Trillions kept falling and building and multiplying. They seemed indestructible.

Meanwhile, Scott taught the Trillions the alphabet and how to form words and obey commands. He knew that if he could communicate with them and prove they were friends, not enemies, he could stop the threat of warfare that might destroy the earth.

Scott reached his goal and established the bridge between humankind and the Trillions.

He could write messages in plain English to them. They could reply, in handwriting made of their own bodies, to him.

Once established, the process rapidly became easier, quicker and more certain. Now they could express thoughts in writing, promptly. And Scott, on fire with excitement, began to find out what they were and what they thought.

"*Trillions, where from?*" he thought and wrote.

The Trillions formed into uncertain shapes. Scott bit his lip. He recognized what was happening. They were "scribbling"—trying to find a right answer, or words in which to put their answer. But at last their reply came.

"*Out there. Sky.*"

"*From a planet?*" Scott wrote.

The Trillions wrote /, which meant Yes. X meant No. ? meant Cannot Reply, or Don't Know. This arrangement saved time.

"*Which planet?*" wrote Scott.

The Trillions promptly replied, "*Home.*"

"Why leave your planet, why come here?" wrote Scott.

"Planet gone," the Trillions replied. Then they began writing again. "Planet die. Explod."

Scott knew that 'explod' meant 'explode'—the Trillions often made spelling mistakes—but he had to have a better answer, so he asked. "Why explode?"

"?"

"Was it a war?"

"X"

"Is the planet gone or is it dead?"

"Dead. Gone. No planet."

Scott had a vision of a dying planet, too old and weak to hold itself together: a planet that had, after countless centuries crumbled, split asunder and broken like a snowball. But the Trillions were writing again...

"X hom for us," appeared on the sheet of white paper. Scott bit his lips, tried to understand.

The Trillions scribbled, then wrote again.

"No hoem for us. Find new hoem."

Now Scott thought he understood. The Trillions had been flung from their planet when it died and broke up. Because they were almost indestructible, they had not died as humans would die. Instead, they had traveled or drifted through space seeking a new home—and had found Earth. He longed to know if their search had been a lengthy one and if they had visited other planets. But there were more important questions. What did they do on their own planet? What were they intending to do on Earth?

So he wrote, "What did Trillions do on home planet?"

"Build," the Trillions replied.

"Build what?"

"As told."

Scott felt his excitement rising.

"Who told you what to build?"

"*Good masters,*" came the answer.

Scott wrote, "*Who were your masters?*"

The Trillions scribbled for a long time, then wrote "*Good at home. Made home good.*"

Scott thought about this. The Trillions found it hard to describe their masters. The best description they could find was, "good"—a word they had used three times. Probably, then, the Trillions had been simple servants under a "master" they could not understand but always obeyed faithfully. He decided to try once more for a description of the masters.

"*Your masters like us?*" he wrote, but got only uneasy scribblings in reply. He decided to try a new tack.

"*Where masters now?*"

"*Dead gone with planet.*"

"*Who tells you what to do now masters gone?*"

There was a great deal of scribbling, then the answer came. "*Build like masters home planet.*"

Perhaps, thought Scott, they mean that as they always built on their home planet, they must build still—it is the only thing they know, the only usefulness they have. He tested this idea by writing, *"Why build?"*

"Like home planet."

Ah, Scott said to himself, I was right. The Trillions were like honeybees—working from habit, working skillfully without reason, working for the sake of the work in obedience to a force they did not need to understand. But, no; this was not good enough. The Trillions were showing intelligence. They were answering his questions. They had learned to write. They were more than blind slaves. They had to have a reason for what they did—a purpose in their visit to Earth.

He wrote, *"Who are your masters now?"*

The Trillions scribbled, began to form a word, scribbled again. At last they wrote, *"Good planet."*

"Am I your master?" Scott wrote.

The Trillions formed a /, then an X, then repeated what they had written before—*"Good planet."*

Scott wrote, *"This planet?"* and the Trillions merely answered with the Yes sign.

Scott sighed. He was more or less back where he had started with the "honeybee" theory—the idea of the blindly obedient workers.

"What will you do for this planet?"

"Build" came the answer. Scott smiled to himself. It was what he had expected.

"What can we do for you?" he wrote.

The answer came back as quickly, violently and directly as a blow in the face.

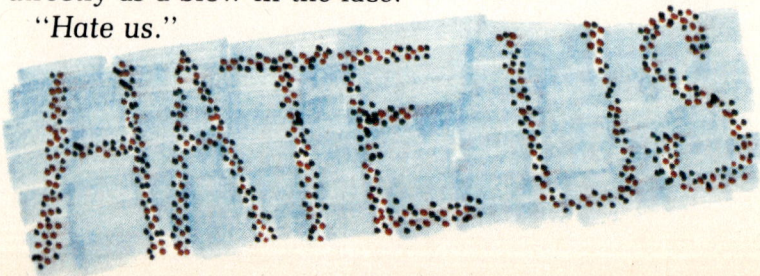

"Hate us."

PART THREE

Trillions, small interlocking jewellike objects, fell from the sky. They formed underwater fortresses and rockets. An international military group decided they were a menace and should be wiped out with Plan A.

Thirteen-year-old Scott was sure Trillions were harmless. He had learned to talk to the Trillions. They told him they had come to Earth from their exploded planet. They wanted to carry on their work of building and repairing. But when Scott asked them, "What can we do for you?" they answered, "Hate us." What did they mean?

Scott and a man called Icarus discuss the Trillions and the strange message. Icarus explains that the Trillions must have been servants of their planet.

"I believe that Trillions worked for the sake of their whole planet—their whole ecology. I believe their planet somehow told them what to do. The side of a mountain collapses, say. A river is diverted. Things—organisms, plants, even animals—that had lived through the river will die. The water they must have to exist is gone. But then the *servants of the planet* are summoned. They form a dam, or new banks, or repair the mountain—they do whatever is needed to restore the river and make things right again."

"They said 'good planet,'" Scott murmured. "That could mean a planet where their masters always had work for them to do. So they built on each other and made whatever the planet needed.... All right—I agree to your theory!" he said. "It's wonderful, marvelous, terrific. But what's the good of it? What difference does it make if you're wrong or right? They don't want to serve us, that's all that matters! They've *told* us so! They told me that they hate us!"

"No, they didn't Scott. They never wrote that," said Icarus. "They didn't say *they* hated *us*. They said—"

"They said we should hate *them*," said Scott, and stopped, baffled.

He could almost feel the answer to the riddle of the Trillions burrowing into his mind. And yet—

"Think, Scott," said Icarus. "Suppose my theory is right—then think. I'll go through it again."

He ticked off his argument point by point on his fingers. "The Trillions exist only to serve the planet, their master. They lose their planet and become like homeless dogs. They find another planet and wish to do the only thing they know—serve, through building. All right so far?"

Scott nodded.

"Then you manage to get through to them. They 'serve' you by learning to write your language. Then comes the important moment. You ask the Trillions what we can do for them—and they answer, 'Hate us.' Now do you see, Scott?"

"No," said Scott miserably.

Icarus looked at his watch and jumped to his feet.

"Come downstairs with me, Scott!" he said. "We'll watch the TV news. Then you'll understand!"

Scott watched but could not concentrate. There was a brief shot of the General saying "No comment" to a group of reporters outside a huge, glassy building. Then brief glimpses of Trillion exterminators in action.

Police with shields and helmets, bursts of flame from petrol bombs. A man in handcuffs being pushed by the police through a crowd, then a shot of the house where murder had been committed. Troops on the border of somewhere or other. A protest march against something or other. A tennis player making a winning smash, a boxer delivering a knockout.

Scott jerked to his feet, eyes wide and staring at Icarus.

"You're right!" gasped Scott. "It must be that. You're right! I was a fool not to have seen it. I mean, we do everything so well. We can build—anything, anything at all. What could they do for us?"

"So the Trillions couldn't compete. On their home planet, they were part of the life of the place—and part of the soul, too. But here—well, humans are too clever. They had to find a job, a task, a reason for being allowed to continue to live here."

" 'Hate us,' " said Scott. "That's a rotten job, just being hated."

"Yes, but what else is there for them? That TV news—for heaven's sake, Scott, what else can they do at this very moment? It's all a fight, Scott—one long battle. Students against police, army against army, nation against nation, boxer hitting another boxer—"

"Punching bag," said Scott thoughtfully. "That's how

the Trillions see themselves. As the punching bag for all our fighting instincts. They know that we never stop fighting. They know that we get better and better all the time at doing each other damage. They must sense that the end is near for this planet—unless we can be switched over to hitting something that doesn't matter and can't be hurt. Though I don't see how that can stop people murdering each other or crashing racing cars."

"It can't," said Icarus. "But don't you see, that's not the part that matters. It's the mass fights that can destroy Earth—the big weapons."

"There'll always be trouble somewhere, I suppose," said Icarus. "Hate. Fighting. Things getting out of balance. Could be that we're our own enemy. But that's the whole point, isn't it? Who are the Goodies, who the Baddies?"

TRILLIONS

(pages 63-74)

1. How did the Trillions communicate with Scott?

2. Why couldn't the Trillions build on our planet as they had on theirs?

3. As what did the Trillions think they could serve us?

4. Look at this TV listing. What channel would Scott be watching in the last part of the story?

   -3- SEE THE PRESS—Discussion
   -5- NEWS—Bruce Hatch
   -6- MOVIE—Comedy
   -9- THE SEARCH—Drama

5. Look at this train schedule. If Scott and Bem left Harbortown on the 6:13 train, what time would they arrive in River Edge?

Cairo	6:05	8:10
Harbortown	6:13	8:18
Duskville	6:27	↓
Rock Falls	7:02	
River Edge	7:20	9:25
Granada	7:45	9:50

ANSWERS

1. They formed letters and shapes with their bodies.
2. The Trillions felt they could not serve us as builders because we were better builders than they.
3. as punching bags and outlets for our fighting instincts
4. Channel 5
5. 7:20

SHADOW OF DEATH

from *They Did It the Hard Way* by Garry Hogg

Alone in the treacherous, freezing wastes of Antarctica after the deaths of his companions, a young explorer, Douglas Mawson, fights desperately to save his own life. Then one false step casts the shadow of death over his head.

He stepped onto a patch of soft snow that was in fact the thin covering of an unseen crevasse. In less time than it takes to tell what happened, he found himself falling down through a blanket of soft, powdery snow and in almost complete darkness. Fortunately he had roped himself to the sled he was hauling, and in spite of the suddenness of the accident had time to realize that his downward motion was slowing, the sled acting as a brake. Even as he dangled there at the end of the harness, he speculated as to whether the sled would reach the lip of the crevasse, topple over and kill him by its sheer weight as it fell vertically down on him.

Strangely, the sled came to a halt, its runners balked by a build-up of soft snow, right on the brink. Mawson found himself revolving slowly at the end of the rope, some twenty feet below the surface. He could see the forward end of the sled almost immediately above him. He estimated the width of the crevasse at about six feet. Its sides were sheer, glass-smooth, so there was no hope whatsoever of being able to climb back up them to the opening. But some six feet or so above his head there happened to be a knot in the rope. He made a superhuman effort and somehow succeeded in struggling up the rope until he could grasp it. He paused to get his breath and then, by a further superhuman effort, which he hardly believed himself capable of, got his feet onto the knot and so was able to reach up and grasp a second knot a yard or so higher up still. By repeating the process he managed at last to spread his arms outward over what remained of the lid. But just as he thought he was about to break free, his foot slipped and the weight thrown on the snow broke it further. Once again he found himself dangling at the full length of the rope which he had so laboriously climbed.

For the first time, as he was to admit later, he not only believed that death was now inevitable, but found himself half wishing that the end might come quickly. Racked by stomach pains, with his feet causing him agony, his body gripped in the noose of rope, its pressure increased by the fact that every pocket and fold of his garments had become filled with loose snow, his hands numb with cold, he heard himself saying that to cut himself free of the harness and plummet into the darkness below his feet would simply be a merciful relief.

Possibly the very thought that he had almost welcomed death frightened him more than the situation in which he now found himself. Anyway, a wave of determination swept through him. He found himself momentarily possessed of what he could recognize even in his present agony of body and mind as truly superhuman strength. He reached once again for the nearest knot in the rope, seized it with an iron grip and hauled himself upward until he could grip it between his knees. He took a fresh grip, got his feet onto the knot and reached for the next one, several feet higher still, as he had done before.

But this time, by some contortion which, he said afterward, he would have believed only a trained acrobat could have achieved, he reversed his position on the rope and succeeded in actually *pushing* himself up the last yard and a half, so that his feet and legs emerged from the crevasse before his head. He bent his legs and rested them cautiously, experimentally, on the lip of the crevasse. Then, forcing himself upward a few inches at a time, he found that he could distribute his weight in such a fashion as not to lay any one part of it too heavily on the fragile snow. Eventually he emerged completely. He had just sufficient strength left to reach for the broken sled and with its help as an anchor, haul himself clear of the crevasse. Then he hauled the sled clear and rolled onto it. There he passed out, utterly exhausted, having saved his life by a maneuver that astonished him afterward whenever he thought about it.

SHADOW OF DEATH

(pages 76-78)

1. Which word would *best* describe how Mawson felt as he was hanging in the crevasse?
   angry   sad   confused   terrified

2. Why did it seem as if there was no hope of climbing up the sides of the crevasse to the top?

3. What frightened Mawson more than the situation in which he found himself?

4. Look at the map of Antarctica. Name the body of water that is closest to Adélie Land.

5. What famous geographical site is near the center of Antarctica?

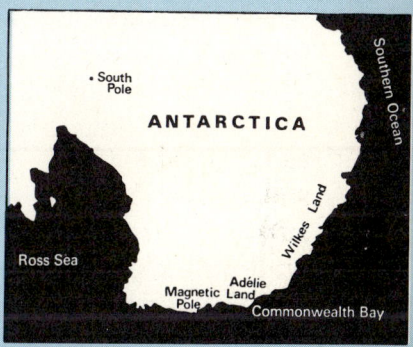

ANSWERS

1. He was angry at his situation, sad over his plight, perhaps confused at first, but most of all he felt *terrified*.
2. The sides were sheer and smooth as glass.
3. the thought that he had almost welcomed death
4. Commonwealth Bay
5. the South Pole

Mind Your Manners

from
*Don't Sit Under
the Apple Tree*
by Robin F. Brancato

Ellie finds out that things haven't changed all that much since the days when her grandmother, Grossie, was a girl. People still carry some things too far—just as they used to.

"Tell me about when you were a girl. About Germany, or about when you and Mary Ellis were in high school."

"Well, let's see," she said. "A short time after I came to America, when we still lived in Philadelphia, Mary and I were invited to a picnic. I was shy then. I didn't speak English so well yet. Mary was already my best friend, and relatives of hers had invited us to go by horse and carriage to a picnic grove down by the river. It was a beautiful day, and all the women at the picnic had brought their own homemade pies and cakes. Each one had tried her hardest to make the most beautiful, best-tasting pastry. There were Bavarian chocolate cakes, and lemon chiffons and cherry pies, but the one I had my eye on was a cake decorated with lovely fresh strawberries. I couldn't wait to be invited to have a piece of that delicious, tempting dessert. But my mother had always told me to be polite, and aside from that, I was, as I say, quite shy."

Grossie was still shy, in a way. I could picture how she must have looked at the picnic. Wearing braids, maybe, and a long dress.

"What happened?"

"Most of the other food was on the table so that every person helped himself or herself, but when the cakes were served at the end, the women who baked them went around to each guest asking who wanted a piece. I was so worried that the strawberry cake would be gone before it was my turn! I turned down all the others, though they looked wonderful too. Meanwhile Mary had already sampled several different ones. Finally, when the woman came to me, there were just two pieces of the strawberry cake left. I remembered my mother's talk about politeness, and I didn't want to sound too eager. 'No thank you,' I whispered to the woman.

"I was sure she would ask me again, because I was the only one with no cake on my plate. But instead, she said 'Poor girl, no appetite!' and went right on by! I could have cried. The next two men on my left each took a piece, and that was the end of the strawberry cake! I was so shy and angry at myself that I didn't even ask for one of the other kinds, even though there were plenty left. I sat and watched Mary and the others smacking their lips and raving over the taste of this one and that, feeling miserable."

"Poor you!" I said.

"To this day whenever I'm offered cake I say yes—but no piece has ever been as good as I had imagined the one at the picnic would be."

She sighed. "Isn't it funny. We learn something—that politeness can be carried too far, for instance—and then we go right on saying to our own children, 'Mind your manners! Wait until you're offered something before you take it! Make sure you don't take too much!' "

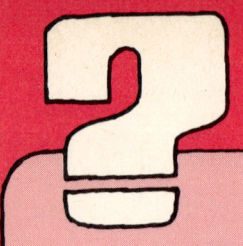

Mind Your Manners

(pages 80-81)

1. What did Grossie learn from her experience at the picnic?

2. What was Grossie's native language?

3. Why did Grossie refuse the cake that she wanted so much?

4. How do you think Grossie felt when there was no second time around?

5. In which magazine would you be more likely to find a story similar to the one you just read?
   - *Home and Family*
   - *National Geographic*

6. If you wanted to find a magazine's monthly food column, you would look in the Table of Contents under _____.
   - Fiction
   - Special Features
   - Regular Features

ANSWERS

1. Politeness can be carried too far.
2. German
3. Grossie didn't want to sound too eager, and she was sure the woman would ask her again.
4. She felt disappointed. Has this ever happened to you?
5. Home and Family
6. Regular Features

UPTOWN HERO

by Nick Pease

This story is based on an event that actually happened in New York City's Central Park.

Officer Lester Nelson was stumped. He was staring glumly at the crowds that had gathered, and at the heavy rescue equipment he'd called in—a tree-trimming lift, a fire truck with an extension ladder, and several electronic megaphones. Then he glared at the top of a large tree again, and from ninety feet up, his quarry—a brilliantly colored South American parrot—glared back.

The previous night the rare bird had somehow escaped from its cage in the Central Park Zoo, and all day long Officer Nelson had been directing recovery efforts. Some of these were ingenious, such as playing tapes of the bird's call through megaphones to entice it to fly down. Others, such as displaying bowls of fruit and nuts, were less original. However, all these attempts had proved futile.

The branch on which the bird was perched was far beyond New York's longest ladder. Then, still pondering, Nelson felt a tug at his coat sleeve. It was that kid again. All afternoon, a slender youth had been begging the officer for a chance to rescue the bird. The boy wore jeans, a denim shirt, and a multicolored cloth cap. Gesturing excitedly, and speaking both Spanish and English, he again asked for a chance to help.

"Okay," thought the weary police officer, "I've tried everything else." He nodded to the youth. He wanted to tell him that the Parks Department would not accept responsibility . . . but he saw the boy wasn't listening. Instead, he was busy taking off his shoes and socks. He quickly stuffed his pockets with fruit and began climbing the tree.

The noisy crowd became hushed, marveling at the young man's agility. Like a monkey he scampered from branch to branch, soon reaching a height of fifty or sixty feet. Just then his cap caught on a twig and came off. Out fell a shower of dark, silky hair. Several people in the crowd gasped. That was no young man in the tree. It was a young woman—Eva Carillo!

By now she was eighty feet up. Her movements became deliberate, and she inched across the last, narrow branch. The parrot eyed her suspiciously. Carefully she drew a banana from her pocket and held it out. Then she began to talk to the bird in a low, soothing voice. The parrot didn't fly off.

Minutes passed, as Eva continued her low, hypnotic cooing. The parrot's fear ebbed. It took a few steps sideways toward the fruit. Hunger and curiosity brought the bird closer to Eva. Now her other arm circled around the bird. Gently her fingers closed upon the bright tail feathers, and the parrot was caught.

A cheer went up from the watching crowd, and the girl picked her way down the tall tree. Her dark eyes sparkled happily as she presented the bird to the zookeepers. The scene was a virtual bedlam—flashbulbs popping, people shaking her hand, reporters thrusting microphones at her. Speaking in breathless Spanish, she gave her name and explained that as a child she had often caught wild parrots in the jungle.

"Where was that?" a reporter asked.

"Uruguay," she responded, and then she stopped, catching herself. Her face clouded over, and she then nervously turned to walk away.

Just then Officer Nelson reached her and began to offer his congratulations. He spoke what little Spanish he knew, but he could see the girl was troubled. Taking her aside, he asked what was upsetting her. She glanced apprehensively at his police officer's badge, but when she looked up into his face she knew she could trust him.

Falteringly, she explained that she had no citizenship papers and no job, and when the news stories got out she might be arrested as an illegal alien. Nelson looked perplexed for a second. Then his features softened, and he told Eva to wait while he made a few phone calls.

Eva waited, sipping a soda, and a few minutes later Nelson returned. He was beaming broadly. "Come with me," he said, taking her by the hand. They returned to the assembled reporters, and Nelson held up his hand for quiet. "Ladies and gentlemen of the press," he said grandly, "I have a few announcements to make. I've just been on the phone with the Mayor, the Parks Commissioner, and the Immigration Service. After hearing about the brave service this young lady has done to New York, they wanted to extend a token of the city's appreciation. First, the Parks Department has offered Ms. Carillo a full-time job. Second, if she decides to accept it,"—the look on Eva's face already said yes—"the Immigration Service has cleared the way for her to become a U.S. citizen. Third, the Mayor has scheduled a banquet in her honor next week. Congratulations, Eva Carillo, and welcome to New York!"

A loud ovation came from the crowd, and the delighted young woman began to step forward to answer all of the reporters' questions. But first she waved good-by to someone on the edge of the crowd. Heads turned to see who it was. It was the large, brilliantly colored parrot. It was being carried off in its cage happily munching on a Brazil nut.

UPTOWN HERO

(pages 83-86)

1. Look up *quarry* in the dictionary. Why was the parrot Lester Nelson's quarry?

2. How did Eva lure the parrot close enough to grab it?

3. What did Eva do after she told a reporter that she used to catch wild parrots in the jungle of Uruguay?

4. Why was Eva afraid to have her name printed in the newspaper?

5. If this story appeared in a newspaper, it would be classified as _____.
   - an editorial
   - a feature story
   - a news story

6. A likely headline for this story would be _____.
   - Mayor Gives Banquet
   - Officer Rescues Girl
   - Girl Rescues Bird

ANSWERS

1. The parrot was the creature that was being hunted.
2. She held out a banana and talked in a low, soothing voice to the bird.
3. Eva stopped talking and turned to walk away.
4. She was afraid she might be arrested as an illegal alien.
5. a feature story
6. Girl Rescues Bird

DOCTOR OF THE MIND

by Nick Pease

Ever had bad days when you were feeling low and everything seemed to turn out wrong? We all have them once in a while. But some people have bad weeks, or even bad months, when nothing they do can make them feel better. Sometimes they go to a special kind of doctor called a psychiatrist. Just as a podiatrist's specialty is the foot, and an osteopath treats bone problems, a psychiatrist treats problems of the mind and the emotions.

Cynthia Benjamin is a psychiatrist. To become a psychiatrist, she had to take pre-med courses in college, go to medical school, spend a year as an intern, and then train for three more years as a psychiatric resident in a hospital. The preparation was long and difficult, but Cynthia thinks it was worth it. She is fascinated by the way the mind works and is glad to be able to help people work out their problems.

The main part of Cynthia's time is spent doing individual therapy, rather than group or family therapy. As a patient sits across from her or lies on a couch, Cynthia asks questions to draw out the person's feelings. Patients may find it hard to talk about personal matters, so Cynthia has to ask the right kinds of questions and has to know how to ask them.

All kinds of people come to Cynthia. Some are constantly unhappy and want to find out why. Others are having upsets with family or friends. A few years ago she saw many young people with bad drug reactions, but now heavy drinking is often the problem. That, she knows, can be just as serious.

Some patients can be helped right away, but for most people therapy is a long process extending over a period of months or years. The results are often gratifying. For example, one high-school girl came to Cynthia because she and her mother couldn't seem to get along. That problem was affecting everything in the girl's life. Although she was very bright, her grades were low and she was losing weight because she had no appetite.

Cynthia worked with the girl for a while, and then met with the girl's mother. Cynthia could tell that the mother had problems of her own, and she referred her to a psychologist. For a couple of years the daughter continued therapy once or twice a week. Gradually she came to understand her own feelings. So did her mother, and they began to feel more comfortable together.

Cynthia feels well rewarded by this human aspect of her work—getting to know her patients and working with them. She controls the impulse she feels to tell her patients what she thinks is wrong, because she knows the patients themselves have to discover this to get the most benefit from her treatment.

A therapist is also very careful not to make judgments about the patients, and everything that is said is held in the strictest confidence. Courts of law cannot demand to see a psychiatrist's records. Trust is very important in psychotherapy. Even with this assurance, some people are uncomfortable about consulting a psychiatrist. They may be afraid of revealing their emotions. Or they may be embarrassed to tell someone what is bothering them.

Cynthia knows that her own learning never stops, so she takes courses in psychoanalysis. These courses help her to investigate the emotions, dreams and fantasies. We know that dreams contain important psychological clues to behavior, so to understand them can help us discover the reasons for a person's actions.

Cynthia is glad to see more opportunities are opening up for women in psychiatry. Now many women are entering different specialties of the field. Some doctors lead group therapy sessions, in which the members of the group help one another with their common problems. Other therapists work exclusively with children—even very young children have been helped by psychiatric counseling.

Cynthia Benjamin enjoys being a doctor of the mind, and she even enjoys many of the jokes about psychiatrists. Here's one that *she* sometimes tells.

Patient: Hello, Doctor, my name is Miss Jones. I've come for psychiatric help. My problem is that people are always forgetting what I say.

Psychiatrist: Very well. Why don't you take a seat, Miss... uh, what did you say your name was?

DOCTOR OF THE MIND

(pages 88-90)

1. What is the job of a psychiatrist?

2. The word *psychotherapy* is easy to understand if you define its two parts. Can you define them?

3. Why doesn't Dr. Benjamin tell her patients what she thinks is wrong with them?

4. Has Dr. Benjamin stopped going to school? How do you know?

5. Read this selection again and time yourself.

6. Another good title for this selection would be _____.
   - Drug Problems
   - A Rewarding Career
   - The Right Kinds of Questions

ANSWERS

1. A psychiatrist treats problems of the mind and the emotions.
2. *Psycho* refers to the mind or "inner life." *Therapy* means the treatment of a disease or disorder. So *psychotherapy* is treatment given to help the mind or the emotions.
3. She knows that the treatment works best when the patients find their own answers.
4. No. She is taking courses in psychoanalysis.
5. Tell your time to your teacher.
6. A Rewarding Career

ACKNOWLEDGMENTS (continued)

"The Duck" on page 55 from VERSES FROM 1929 ON, by Ogden Nash. Copyright 1936 by Ogden Nash. Reprinted by permission of Little, Brown and Company and of J.M. Dent and Sons.

"The Camel" on page 55 from VERSES FROM 1929 ON, by Ogden Nash. Copyright 1933 by The Curtis Publishing Company. Reprinted by permission of Little, Brown and Company and of J.M. Dent and Sons.

Selection on page 57 from A TIME FOR WATCHING, by Gunilla Norris. Copyright © 1969 by Gunilla Norris. Reprinted by permission of Alfred A. Knopf, Inc. and of Curtis Brown, Ltd.

Selection on page 63 from TRILLIONS, by Nicholas Fisk. Copyright © 1971 by Nicholas Fisk. Reprinted by permission of Pantheon Books, a division of Random House, Inc. and of Hamish Hamilton Children's Books Ltd.

Selection on page 76 from THEY DID IT THE HARD WAY: SEVEN ASTOUNDING JOURNEYS. Copyright © 1973 by Garry Hogg. Reprinted by permission of Pantheon Books, a division of Random House, Inc. and of Abelard-Schuman Limited.

Selection on page 80 from DON'T SIT UNDER THE APPLE TREE, by Robin F. Brancato. Copyright © 1975 by Robin F. Brancato. Reprinted by permission of Alfred A. Knopf, Inc.

Photo Credits

Photo on page 28 by S.C. Bisserot/Bruce Coleman, Inc.
Photo on page 29 by David Overcash/Bruce Coleman, Inc.
Photo on page 36, "The Fall of Icarus" by Pieter Brueghel, The Bettmann Archive, Inc.
Photo on page 37, "The Harvesters" by Pieter Brueghel, the Elder, from The Metropolitan Museum of Art, Rogers Fund, 1919
Photo on page 50 from The Metropolitan Museum of Art, Purchase, Florance Waterbury bequest and gift of Mr. and Mrs. Nathan Cummings, by exchange, 1973
Photo on page 51 from The Metropolitan Museum of Art, Gift of the Citizen's Committee for the Army, Navy and Air Force, 1962

Illustrations by Publishers Graphics

Every effort had been made to trace the ownership of all copyrighted material in this book and to obtain permission for its use.